# Selfish

## is a

# Superpower

## Jessica Dennehy

**WORDS MATTER**
P U B L I S H I N G
OUR WORDS CHANGE THE WORLD

Words Matter Publishing
P.O. Box 1190
Decatur, IL 62525
www.wordsmatterpublishing.com

Cover photo cred: 7 Seconds Media

ISBN: 978-1-958000-64-9

Library of Congress Catalog Card Number: 2023940214

# Dedication

To the three best friends who gave me permission to become who I was meant to be and blindly supported me through that transformation. I told you I would change our lives. ♥ I love you more than vacations...more than Doritos...more than the universe.

And, to all the women who were told they had to choose between being an incredible mom, living an adventurous life, or having a successful career. We are about to shatter that glass ceiling...

# Table of Contents

# *Prologue*

---

# Please Proceed Only If You'd Like to Have it All

# Introduction

The first thing you need to know about me is: My daughters and I are close. Like super close. Like, we even have a theme song that marks our place in the world as: The Three Best Friends.

This MUST be the first thing you learn about me because then it will all make sense.

You will know that the rest of this book are words that come from a deeply meaningful place where parenthood plays an enormous role.

You will know that I absolutely love being a mom. I care about my daughters more than anyone else on this planet. And they are the brightest spot in my life.

But they are not everything.

They used to be.

But that is when my life fell apart. That is when I lost any semblance of myself.

To pick the pieces back up, I had to do something extremely scary.

To elevate my life, I had to put a love for myself before a love for them.

And that terrified me.

We are taught that this is the opposite of what any loving parent...especially a mother...should do.

But I'm here to tell you, "F" those people. They are wrong. And they don't know the first thing about parenting while also creating a business empire or a life that you not only LOVE but also LIVE.

I—on the other hand—do.

And I'm going to share with you the way that I have grown my personal and professional life into something amazing while also being the most present, fun, loving, and meaningful parent I could be.

When I think about sacrifice, I know that in my heart, I will not sacrifice the way I parent for anything. I knew I had to create a life that would allow me to be the type of mother I wanted to be while also being the type of insanely successful businesswoman I also wanted to be.

I wanted it all. And the fact that "everyone" said I couldn't have it made me want to fight for it even more.

That's the thing about me. When my heart is set on something, I'm going to find a way to make it happen. Naysayers just add fodder to my fire and set my passion ablaze even further. Because anytime someone told me I couldn't or shouldn't, that is when I knew I was doing the EXACT thing I was meant to be doing.

Instead of listening to a bunch of talking heads who could only attain success in one part of their life, choosing between building a career or a family, take advice from someone who has been able to live the life they preach...the life you wish for.

Take advice from someone who has grown a successful business, travels the country to speak on stages, and has written three books while also doing every drop-off, pick-up, project, and playdate: while also volunteering at school, being on the board of the PTA, and running book fairs. While also traveling the world to create memories with my kids and living life to the absolute fullest. Oh, and did I mention I am also a single mom?

I am not a parenting expert. Heck, I am not even a business expert in. I am a constant work in progress, learning more and more with every mistake, every trial, and every error.

Even after growing five successful businesses and raising two daughters alone for the past seven years (and counting), I am still not an expert.

I am still learning and evolving into the best parent and businesswoman I can be. I am still learning better ways, tweaking my flaws, and revising the way I show up. I am still learning to love myself, give myself grace, cheer myself on, and be open to more of what the world has to offer.

But what I can offer you is all of the strategies I have used to light up my life and make it the amazing life I know and love today. It is still imperfect, but it is mine, and it makes me insanely happy on all levels.

Pouring into these pages as we speak is lighting me up because I know...I KNOW...that so many of you will read it and find that ray of hope you need to believe YOU can do it. You can have it all. You can maintain your own autonomy while still being an amazing mom. You can get selfish and pour into yourself without messing up your kids' lives. You can go out and be the career woman you've only dreamed of being without the guilt and dread that society tries to lay on us for dreaming big.

What I hope for you is that this book gives you the courage to take just one step in the direction of your dreams. And then, you reach out to me to tell me all about it.

So, buckle up because I am about to blow the lid off every single lie you've ever been told. And we're gonna have some Thelma and Louise-style fun as YOU run this car right off a damn cliff into the life of your dreams!

Time to see why Selfish is actually a Superpower.

# *Part 1*

---

# Life Before I Got Selfish

# Chapter 1

L et's rewind.

One day I woke up and was a mom. It's probably the one moment in life where you wake up in an instant and have totally morphed from someone you recognized into someone who is absolutely nothing like the person twenty-four hours prior.

If you don't have kids yet, you won't believe me. But keep reading anyways. It's the kind of thing you can't really understand until it's happened to you. It sounds outrageous, and we all try to convince ourselves that we will somehow be the one woman in the world that parenthood doesn't have this effect on. It's hilarious! But, live on in your bubble until it happens to you. We get it...We've all been there!

Any who, I digress. One day I woke up, and I had zero clue who the heck I was anymore.

Up until that point, my whole life had been focused on becoming an attorney, traveling, and having highly intellectual conversations about art, literature, history, and all the brainy things I love. I kept this up even while pregnant, so I figured if the pregnancy hadn't gotten the best of me, surely, I would remain unaffected by a tiny human in my arms.

Wrong.

That tiny human changed my life in a lot of amazing ways. But like all other gifts from the universe, you have to go through some pretty crummy times before you get to all the amazing goodness of enjoying the miracles we manifest.

At the time I had Emma, I was a Wall Street attorney that was in love with her job. It was something I had strived for, and it did not disappoint. It was fast-paced and intellectually stimulating, and I was protecting investors, which at the time felt valiant for a lawyer.

I was also happily married to the love of my life. We had a pretty blissful marriage thus far. We were about four years in, traveled several times a year, loved each other's company, and had some amazing things to talk about. We were really in love, and up until that point, I was a good wife.

But when I held Emma in my arms for the first time, that former life I loved so much fell away in an instant, and the only thing I wanted was to make sure I gave her an amazing life full of opportunity and magic.

In my head, it seemed like a natural thing to want for your child, especially as a first-time parent. But in retrospect, this was the beginning of a co-dependent way of life that I came to think was totally normal until everything fell apart.

It isn't Emma's fault, of course. Hell, it's not even my fault. Having a baby is hard on the mind, body, and soul. I was learning how to navigate a completely different phase of life with completely different emotions, all while recovering physically and emotionally from a nine-month pregnancy and the aftermath. I was doing the best I could in that situation, and I forgive myself for not doing life perfectly at that point.

In fact, I wouldn't change a single thing because the series of events that unfolded have made me who I am today, and right now, life is pretty beautiful and amazing. But it took a lot of heartaches to get there, so if this story can get you to the good part even a smidge faster than I got there, that makes this book worthwhile.

The months after I had Emma were filled with joy. Some women would probably be cooking for their hubbies while they're home, making sure the house is spotless, and caring for the baby. But instead, I decided to make the most present time out of my six-month maternity leave. Emma and I made some amazing memories at the pool, at the beach, and with my mom. She also helped her father and I as we built our very first business the same week she was born: MadMen Barbershop. We wanted it to open halfway through my maternity leave so that we could have it built out and running before I went back to work (for more about the story around my business build-out, refer to my first book: *Pivot & Slay*).

A lot went on during those first six months of her little life. And I distinctly remember the night before I went back to work.

Emma was cradled in my arms in a rocking chair my mother used when I was a child. I was gently rocking her back and forth, telling her how much I loved her. And tears were pouring down my face. That may seem standard to you, but for me, it is unusual. I am not a crier. I do not cry easily, even after having my kids, even during pregnancy, and even as a mom.

That night I cried because the thought of leaving her and going back to my job was unbearable. (Side note: I often think, man, how do people who hate their jobs go back if I had such a hard time going back to a job I actually loved?).

I remember my husband walking into the nursery, startled by the fact I was balling my eyes out. He asked what was wrong, and I looked up at him and cried: "Please tell me I don't have to go back tomorrow; tell me I can stay home, and you can make this business work, so I don't have to leave her.

His eyes showed massive concern at this point because my true nature is to be a career woman. I had always loved having a successful career, traveling into NYC, and working my dream job. I never once mentioned staying home to raise kids. It wasn't something I ever wanted, ever. So, he was quite surprised at this moment of vulnerability and despair. He probably would have been less surprised at that point if I had said, "Please shave my head."

Of course, I went back to my career the next day. There was no choice (yet). One thing all new businesses need is a constant stream of capital. How would we ever make MadMen a huge success if I didn't go back to work to help fund the shop, the house, the baby, and every other facet of our life? Deep down, I knew I had to go, but it was a painful moment, nonetheless.

Having my first child and then returning to work marked the beginning of the end of life as I knew it. From that moment forward, the things that used to light me up—my marriage, my dream job, and the things I enjoyed as Jessica—paled in comparison to the way I lit up when I was with my daughter. I lost sight of my marriage, who I was at my core, what I wanted for myself, and what I needed to keep my happiness. And my not-so-secret identity became: Supermom.

Emma lit me up. I loved being around her. She was curious about everything, never in a bad mood, and had endless enthusiasm like me. We were two peas in a pod. Even experiencing the most mundane tasks, like grocery shopping, turned into a big, exciting adventure for us.

Feeling guilty that I had to work longer hours as a lawyer, I made up for it by being super present with Emma when I got home. I wouldn't let anyone feed her dinner so that I could do it. I wanted to be the one to give her a bath, read her a book, and put her to bed every night. On the weekends, I'd be endlessly devoted to her. We still had our new business to tend to, so my husband would take care of all that when I got home from work and on the weekends.

In my mind, things were going really well. But in reality, everything was slowly starting to fall apart. I felt too guilty to get a babysitter after working all week, so I didn't want to do date nights anymore and wouldn't see my friends very often. I ditched my gym membership and bought some equipment for my home so I wouldn't have to run out, but my routine was still lacking because I was so drained from being a working supermom.

In fact, I gave up all of the things that brought me joy before becoming a mother so that I could make sure to be the best mom I could be. That's what society tells us, right? "Put the kids first; do what they need; no more time to be selfish now that you're a mom."

Well, I call BS because that entire belief system is what made my life break down. If someone had told me the truth, maybe the road to my transformation may have been a little easier.

Life went on in this manner for quite some time. I loved being a mom so much that I wanted another baby asap, not realizing how much harder two humans are (even though it's so obvious now!). At age 31, my doctors told me I wouldn't be able to have another baby, and that type of devastation created another level of pressure on my already-strained marriage.

So much had happened since having Emma. MadMen was totally flourishing, which left my husband super busy inside of the business; with me working as a lawyer full-time at a job I was slowly starting to hate. He and I weren't consistently spending time alone or working on our marriage, so we kept growing further and further apart. He was neck deep in some serious entrepreneurial issues that I couldn't quite understand yet because that was so far from my journey at a "9-5" corporate job. Our inability to connect on that level caused a lot of tension, as did the business's constant need for capital which was difficult on a saver like me. (Side note: it's funny now, having had my own entrepreneurial journey unfold, I can really see so much of his side of the story more clearly than I could at the moment.)

Meanwhile, I had zero life outside of lawyering and mom-ing. I never did anything for myself, a trap many parents fall into. I was literally on a hamster wheel at work and at home. And spending every spare moment I could making up for my fallacies as a working mom to spend time with my daughter, who I was convinced would grow up to hate me if I operated any other way.

Sound familiar yet?

Then we added infertility to our list of woes, and things went off the rails. My husband and I were so stressed out, which made everyone's life exponentially harder.

One of the hardest moments in my life was when doctors told me that I had a almost no chance of conceiving a baby that was genetically mine. In the scheme of things, there are worse issues. I was a healthy thirty-one-year-old with a thriving career and business, a loving marriage, a beautiful home, and one healthy child. Things could be a lot worse. But at the moment, I felt totally devastated and hopeless.

It was difficult to wrap my head around the "reality" that this could not happen. Western medicine said so, but remember what I do when someone tells me no? I go at it harder and more creatively than before to prove them wrong. In this particular instance, tenacity and creativity moved mountains. For the first time in my life, I left the logical part of myself behind and jumped fully into my emotional and spiritual side.

I use the word spiritual because I am not what mainstream society would identify as religious. If you haven't figured it out yet, I don't much like authority. I like to operate in a way that's meaningful to me, and that doesn't always include conforming to societal norms. Religion is one of the norms I haven't embraced in a traditional way.

To me, religion is fascinating from a historical standpoint. I love the theology of it and the reasoning behind its formation throughout the creation of the modern world. I've read a lot about various religions. Through the years, I've picked up bits and pieces from each, the parts I feel connected to, whether they go together or not.

My infertility was the start of my own little spiritual journey, which I still hold near and dear today: healing stones. Some people call them crystals or even precious gems. Whatever you call them or believe, one thing is clear. They are pretty, and who doesn't want something pretty when they're feeling down?

My mom knew how sad I was about the infertility news, so to cheer me up, she bought me the best gift ever. Still, to this day, this is THE most meaningful gift anyone has ever gotten me. Ever. Period.

It was a small carnelian crystal. My first healing stone and the one that first introduced real magic into my life.

If you don't believe in magic, that's fine. Although I'm sure with my brilliant lawyering skills, I can create an evidentiary locker filled with moments in your life where you've experienced magic. Even just the miracle of your body growing a human inside of it is magic, in my humble opinion.

Regardless, this was magic to me. Mainly because it defied all logic. As an attorney, my life was based on logic. So, for me to go off the grid and purely based on instinct and emotion, believing in the healing properties of this carnelian stone was a HUGE deviation from my norm.

But here I was, gripping this stone every single day, wishing for a miracle. My own form of prayer.

This stone is said to help with fertility. Who am I to disagree? If Western medicine is telling me I can't have a baby, maybe I don't want to believe in it anymore...at least for this moment in time. So, I hold the stone in my hand, look up at the stars and pray for a miracle. Then I throw it in my bra and go on with my day. Bra Rocks. It's a thing.

(Side note...one time during yoga, the rocks fell out of my bra and banged loudly on the floor. I came out of my pose to retrieve them and knew I had found my people. Not one person in that room thought it was odd. After class, everyone told me stories about their bra rocks slipping out at the most awkward times.)

After three months of carrying this stone around, guess what happened? I saw the strongest heartbeat on a monitor in the doctor's office. Emma was sitting on my lap, my husband was next to me, and I was overcome with emotion. That little stone changed my entire life. Because it gave me hope. And hope is a magical thing.

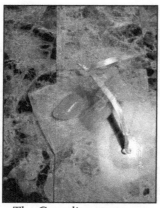

The Carnelian stone my mom gave me.

Me in Nantucket, 6 months pregnant with Quinn. 2013

Emma excited to be a big sister. 2013

# Chapter 2

I wished and wished and wished for her. And there she was. My tiny miracle. A miracle I still thank the universe for every single day (the universe and Natalie Portman's dad, who was my fertility specialist! Even he was surprised that I got pregnant naturally!)

Quinn came into the world as a force to be reckoned with, and she still tests the boundaries of the world every day, which is something I really love about her.

That's not the only time a crystal changed my life. I often use them when I am struggling to accomplish something. Not because I think they are magic (ok...well, maybe *I* do, but you don't have to!), but because they are a gentle daily reminder of what I need to do to create the life I want.

In that first example, it was literal life that was created. And her little life was chaos from the start, so I should have seen it all coming...right?

Getting pregnant with Quinn was traumatic for all of us. I was an emotional wreck thinking I would never have another biological child, which stressed out my husband and put a lot of pressure on him. I'm sure Emma felt all that tension because she started to seem anxious too. But the pregnancy flew by, and before we knew it, we were a family of four. I had always dreamed of having four girls, and now I was halfway there, and likely that is where I would stay. The doctors said this was the end of the road for me, and I had more or less accepted that as I held Quinn for the first time and really felt a wholeness as a family that I hadn't felt before. I was extremely grateful that I was blessed with two healthy babies.

Quinn made quite an entrance into this world. The doctors thought I had time because my contractions were far apart, even though I kept telling them I didn't. But what do I know? I'm just the one feeling all the things....delivering a baby.

Well, within twenty minutes of arriving at the hospital, she was born, before they could even set us up in a proper delivery room ready; before they could administer me any medicine. They had nowhere to put her, so they plopped her on my chest as she wailed. But the second they placed her down, she looked up at me, stopped crying, and passed out.

My feelings exactly.

If I thought I had lost myself before, things were only about to take another dip entirely.

Two kids are no joke. In my opinion, it is even harder than becoming a parent for the first time. The first time you are clueless and worried about every little thing, but you have time to overthink things and figure it out.

Two kids are terrifying because you know how hard one is, and then you realize (when it's far too late) that you've just decided to do it all again, except this time, the first tiny human is still wanting and needing you every second of the day too.

When I talk about this moment in my life with other parents and how much it took out of me personally, they all seem to understand. They say the same thing happened to them; that having kids is hard, that it really tests a marriage.

The difference is most of them didn't lose their marriage after having one of the most amazing precious gifts handed to them.

The juxtaposition of the highest high and the lowest low was a bizarre thing to experience. Just as I held my miracle baby and was basking in the glory of getting my wish, that is when my marriage took a sharp turn into the abyss.

Now, when I talk about my marriage, don't get bent out of shape. This book is about me and my journey, so I am going to talk a lot about the things I now take responsibility for in the demise of the relationship.

That isn't to say I am fully to blame. Of course, I am only 50% of the marriage and, therefore, 50% of the problem. But this book isn't about him, so I will focus on where I went wrong so you can see how helpful it can be to put yourself under a microscope. Not with an eye towards judgment, but with an eye towards EVOLUTION!

You see, I could have chosen to blame the downfall of our marriage on a lot of things outside of my control...business or motherhood or hormones, or my husband's mistakes. But instead, I chose to take a deeper look at the things I could have done better so that I could evolve and avoid making the same mistakes over and over again.

I'm a firm believer that the universe (that is what I call the powers that be ...you can substitute the word for whatever fits your belief system) presents the same issues to you in different ways over and over until you finally learn the lesson.

Some people will never learn. They'll go through this life repeating the same mistakes again and again in different relationships, scenarios, jobs, etc. And they will never understand why "this keeps happening to them."

I don't want you to be one of those people.

I want you to be the person that understands: life happens FOR you, not TO you.

Life wants you to learn. It tries to set up the perfect scenario for you to see the light. But as the saying goes: you can bring a horse to water, but you can't make it drink.

There is only one thing that will help you learn the lesson: Awareness. That is all. It is a simple notion, but it is not an easy thing to accomplish.

The first thing you need to know is that circumstances create a perfect storm that then leads you down a certain path. But ultimately, you CAN stop the crazy train. You can choose differently. Most of you just don't realize how much control we have until it's too late, myself included.

I was skipping through life, completely oblivious to the storm brewing around me. I'm not judging myself. I had a lot on my plate. MadMen had totally taken off. Juggling two kids was wearing on me, and then I had double the mom guilt for working so much and even less energy to put into my marriage.

The real heartache came from my job. I was becoming increasingly frustrated by something that used to bring me a lot of excitement and pride. I felt like I had hit the ceiling super hard and had nowhere to go. The positions above me were not the ones I wanted because I didn't get to do the work I really enjoyed. I already maxed out my potential at my current position. I had tried some amazing cases and investigated a ton of others. I didn't feel excited by the work anymore. It felt routine and mundane. Sometimes I would look around the office and realize I didn't fit in anymore. I was the only person with any ambition or drive to do more.

Everyone else was super happy coasting along in a job that was predictable. Predictability was something they coveted. They enjoyed knowing their salary and benefits were secure. They reveled in the fact that they had done the same job so many times they could do it upside down with their eyes closed. They were comfortable, and they liked it that way. And there is absolutely nothing wrong with that.

Except, it wasn't for me anymore.

Before kids, I had been the person who was risk adverse. Opening up a business was the most stressful thing because we could have lost it all, or we could have become millionaires. At that time, I preferred the stability of a corporate job.

But the more MadMen took off and the more I saw my husband lit up about it, the more I yearned to feel like that about something. And my Wall Street job was definitely not that something.

I am a passionate person. I want to feel lit up and excited the majority of the time. I want to be doing things that make me feel like I am lighting the world on fire and I want the people around me to have that same excited feeling, even if it isn't about the exact same stuff that I feel excited about.

The problem was, I had lost my identity so much, I had no clue what lit me up anymore. I was a shell of the fiery person I used to be. My life revolved around doing my mundane job and then rushing home to be a super mom. There was nothing in between.

Frustration was an understatement. I was feeling depressed, but even more than that, angry. Angry that I wasn't happy at work, but I also didn't know what else to do. Angry that MadMen was lighting up my husband, and I couldn't figure out how to do that for myself. So I started getting frustrated with him instead. Looking back, I know it was a projection. He was doing something he loved, but it only made us grow further apart. He was getting happier, and I was getting angrier.

At the time, I didn't understand it. But I now know I was upset because I didn't know what the heck I wanted. I just knew I was unhappy, and I kept focusing on that feeling, which only made me more unhappy. You get what you focus on.

I hated being at work. I loved being home with the girls but also didn't want to ONLY do that. I just finished my six-month maternity leave after having Quinn, and as much as I loved being with my girls, I knew that I couldn't ONLY be a mom. I needed something else, something intellectually stimulating. I needed to push my career forward.

I wanted it all: a crazy successful career and also to be an influential and meaningful parent. I just couldn't figure out how to have both.

My marriage wasn't even on my radar at that time because I was so consumed with figuring out the other two pieces, and frankly, I took my marriage for granted. We had such a strong relationship before the birth of our kids; I just assumed that even if we coasted through the earlier stages of their childhood, we would be ok. I thought I could let that part of my life ride out while I figured out the other parts, but I couldn't have been more wrong.

He saw the issues long before I did. He felt alone and left out of the relationships I was creating with the kids. It was almost like it was me and the girls and then him. This wasn't intentional. I actually loved him very, very much. But as I said, I was feeling so many emotions around being miserable at work and mom guilt. I was in a maze and couldn't figure my way out.

MadMen had totally taken off (more about that in my first book). Knowing that I didn't love my job anymore, my husband suggested that I leave. Financially we could finally float it. We wanted to expand MadMen, and it would be helpful to have both of us working in the business as we expand and would give us more flexibility so I could also have more time with the girls. And part of us believed that we could spend more time together and regain the connection we lost.

I was scared. Being an attorney was part of my identity, and I was already losing so much of my identity during this crazy phase of life. But he was right—I was miserable. And maybe leaving would give me an opportunity to figure out what would actually make me happy.

But as we all know: if you want something different, you have to do something different. So, I took the plunge. I left Wall Street and went all in on the business and family.

Looking back, it's almost like when people decide to have a baby to save their marriage. It never works out.

Similarly, neither did this.

I mean, in some ways, it worked out. Without this pivotal moment in time, I wouldn't be the woman you see today.

Seven years ago, I hadn't even written one book…let alone two. I never spoke on stage before. I didn't own and operate four different businesses. I didn't drive a fancy car. I had never flown on a private jet. I didn't own a consulting company or know how to help other entrepreneurs achieve success. I hadn't been featured in prestigious magazines like Forbes or met any celebrities. Heck, seven years ago, I couldn't even figure out my own mess, let alone help anyone else.

But that moment was the beginning of my transformation into a better, stronger, more secure human being. And just like any other Level Up moment, I had to crash really hard before I got to the good part.

My first day as an attorney at
the New York Stock Exchange. 2006

Me snuggling my
little miracle, 2014

Chili's was the site of one of my most memorable family moment. We didn't even eat there much, but Emma really wanted to go that night, so we did.

We sat at a secluded table, and I said, "I have some big news."

Emma is an old soul. At the time, she was three and a half years old but acted like she was 7.

She looked up at me, "OoooOOO, what is it, Mommy?"

And I told her, "I'm not going to have to go to work anymore. I'm only going to work at MadMen so I can be with you girls more."

She stared at me. Her eyes filled up with tears, and she threw her entire body into me, clutching me tight. She sobbed, "THANK YOU, MOMMY, THANK YOU!"

It was one of the best moments of my life. We even have a picture to commemorate it, and even today, Emma has it framed on her desk.

I have to admit; it felt good to have her want me around that much because, like all parents, we know how fleeting those moments are. One day, they'll be off doing their own thing, not thinking much about us at all, let alone yearning for our presence.

But here was a three-year-old who was beyond grateful to get even more of my love and affection than she already had, and I was elated that I could give that to her.

My husband had other things in mind. He wanted to have our babysitter come an extra one or two times a week in addition to the time she came so we could work to allow us time to go on a weekly date.

But I didn't want to commit.

How crazy is that? I didn't want to commit to keeping my marriage healthy. I was in my own bubble dreaming about how amazing of a mom I could be now that I was home more, and I didn't want to dedicate the time to make my marriage more interesting or better.

It wasn't just my marriage I was neglecting. It was also myself. I didn't even want to get a babysitter to give me some free time to go to the gym or do yoga, both of which I loved.

I was all in on the motherhood route, and I had blinders on to anything that didn't revolve around that. I was lost. I had zero sense of self. Zero sense of style (I hadn't shopped in ages). Zero sex drive. And my former zest for career and travel had really been hampered by parenting.

I know you all feel me. This is the most common problem I hear from career women. They are so busy playing all the roles they entirely forget to play the role of themselves. You forget you are a person too. And the role of YOU is the most important role you can ever play. Yet, you put it on the backburner as if it doesn't matter at all.

That's what I did too. At that moment in time, the only thing that brought me joy was my daughters. My former career as an attorney no longer lit me up. My husband was lit up by our business, which made me jealous because he found a passion, and I couldn't. He talked about work and thought about work nonstop, which I found mundane. I spoke about the kids nonstop, which he found mundane. And round and round we went. The more aware I became of all of this, the more I threw myself into being a mom because it made me happy, and I was good at it. So the cycle perpetuated.

Finally, my husband suggested we open a second shop, and we were able to funnel some energy into looking for a space. This briefly brought a spot of light into our energy.

We had fun running around together, scouting out empty commercial spaces, and having lunch. It gave us some common ground to talk about for a month or two until we finally found a place we loved. I got to negotiate the lease, which was in my wheelhouse and gave me a sense of purpose inside the business.

I hadn't quite gotten my footing at MadMen. Prior to this, I really played the role of investor and wife. I funded the business and was a sounding board for when he needed to vent, strategize or get creative. But I had no role day-to-day because I was working on Wall Street. Now with opening another shop, the plan was for me to be more involved.

Maybe this would be the thing that brought us closer together. At that point, I didn't really have an interest in running the shops. I didn't feel particularly passionate about haircuts, and the shop's brand personality was my husband's, not mine. So naturally, he felt more connected to the brand than I did. But I had so much fun scouting for a new location that I thought maybe this would give me some energy to figure out what the heck I wanted.

Lease negotiations went well, and we signed a ten-year commitment in March 2016. Life felt great. We were ready to take over the barbering world and create an empire.

Only three weeks later, instead of taking over the world, our world would implode, and we would decide to sever our marriage.

Bad timing, right? Our lease included three months rent-free so that we could build-out the shop without having to pay rent. We had ninety days to open this baby up for business before we owed a ton of money, and we were intent on opening much faster—a month before our first rent was due. What a time to have a marriage fall apart just as we were about to be locked in a 2200-square-foot space painting and decorating for sixty days.

Shortly after signing the lease, we decided to end it. I think it was actually weeks before I told anyone anything because I was just in shock.

Looking back, I shouldn't have been. It was obvious we weren't really in love anymore, at least not in the way married people *should* be. I guess I thought that this was just a phase marriages go through. It was an ebb and flow, and eventually, we'd flow through it.

Guess not.

If you had told me then that one day this moment in time wouldn't even matter, I would never have believed you. At the moment, it felt huge. Unbearable. Embarrassing.

But now, I know better.

Our separation and ultimate divorce were pretty painful. The hardest part about that wasn't the judgment but the fact that I was already having a tough time establishing my place and purpose inside the business. I started on this journey as a shell of the person I used to be. Already broken down by a lack of purpose and passion. A little lost soul looking for a home that embodied more than just being a mom.

And now here I was—a stranger in my own business, having to figure out my place in the world and inside of MadMen while simultaneously grieving the painful loss of my marriage.

Broken was an understatement. But as they say, the sky is darkest right before dawn.

The girls as we did construction inside our 2nd MadMen location. 2016

# *Part 2*

---

# Redefining Selfish

# Chapter 4

It's important to note that without this divorce, I may not have ever found myself. Life is like that. When you refuse to make a change necessary to push your life forward, sometimes life will just come at you hard and try to knock some sense into you.

This divorce was that moment for me. The universe previously had been only handing me gentle nudges. But the Sicilian in me was too thick-headed and maybe a tad naïve to see it.

Challenge accepted.

It was now time to totally rip out the rug from under myself so that I could see the light, get my act together and build the life of my dreams. I just didn't know it yet.

That is why years later, I am grateful for this immense learning opportunity that exposed the deepest darkest insecurities I had, all with an eye towards releasing me from them.

Often times we go through life hiding things we are ashamed of or insecure about. We think if we don't speak about them or acknowledge their existence, they'll simply go away, when in fact, this only makes them more powerful. You can only remove their power by talking about it. Admitting to it. Fessing up to your part in the demise of your career, relationship, or life.

It took me far too long to realize that, so I hope this saves you some time. I spent many, many months ignoring the reality of my life. I thought parenting and juggling a career were hard. But now, here I was, parenting two kids alone and navigating how to run a business with two locations while my entire personal life was falling apart.

To parent in the best way, you have to really know yourself first. This gives you the awareness to understand all the different parts of you and use them in unique combinations to parent each child differently, depending on what they need.

To run successful businesses, you really have to know yourself well. Then you can infuse your energy into the brand and into the leadership you emanate.

To have a successful life, you really need to know yourself well. When you know yourself well, you can rule your life with enthusiasm and direction.

Well, in 2016, I had exactly none of those traits.

I was steering the ship entirely alone without any sense of self. It became abundantly clear that I had lost my entire identity first by identifying as a Wall Street attorney and letting my self-worth be based on my career, then by identifying as a mom and letting my self-worth be based on parenting.

I knew I was lost, but I couldn't find the willpower to ask for help because that required me to admit that I had no idea who I was, and that hurt too much.

Not utilizing my friends and family for the moral support that I so desperately needed, I became a recluse. There were only two places I went during those months: to MadMen, trying to find my footing as a business owner and leader, and to the beach to cry my eyes out. People probably thought I had lost my mind. Our babysitter made me leave the house because the girls worried about me too much hearing me cry. So instead, I ugly cried at the beach. I would straight up wail on a public bench at the boardwalk.

No shame in my game. I needed to release all of that pent-up hurt and pain. In my mind, I was 1000% failing as a mom. All my dreams of leaving my career to be a super mom were flying out the window because I couldn't stop crying. I couldn't parent. Couldn't think. Couldn't even get angry because I was too sad.

The messy stage lasted several months, and really the only thing that kept me from total demise was MadMen. The thing I originally had little passion for became the thing that kept my mind sharp, occupied my energy, and became a positive drive and challenge in my life. I didn't know it at the time, but MadMen was slowly saving me and also laying the foundational groundwork for who I was about to become: a better leader, a happier human, and the bada$$ I am today.

But like any good come-up story, we first have to start with all the fear and angst. That's the hardest part of success and also a necessary evil to invite all of the things you want into your life.

We all know if you want something different, you have to do something different. But that is scary as hell. I was walking into the unknown without a flashlight because I had to learn to be my own guiding light. I had to learn to be my own lightbulb and shine that onto the path before me.

All this time, I was waiting for some outside source to come into my life and light me up; to give me the happiness I had been longing for. But my journey through divorce and business ownership allowed me to realize that I am that source. I MUST BE THAT SOURCE.

When you are the source of your own happiness, your life cannot rise and fall with outside circumstances. The only thing that your happiness depends on is you. How empowering is that?

We walk around life allowing these external things to control our mood. To control our outcomes. To control the way our day goes. But really, we have the power to change all of that. To be affected or unaffected by all of these things outside of our control. We have the power to control whether something puts us into a tailspin or we choose to overcome it, ignore it, or face it.

That's a choice. And once you are aware of that, you gain back all the power over your life.

Awareness is the most powerful tool you can cultivate in your life. It is the key that allows you to be a better person, parent, leader, and spouse. The only way to gain awareness of self is to be with yourself. To sit in that stillness that is painstakingly quiet. To be mundane, routine, and introspective until it no longer becomes uncomfortable. Allow all your insecurities to bubble to the top so you can face them head-on instead of running from them and letting them run you.

The quiet sucks at first, but then it becomes addicting because you know it will give you the clarity you need to make epic stuff happen!

We'll save the epic stuff for later, but just know that this will be the result of the hard work you do in between the tragedy and the success.

The middle is the muck. It's the part where you take a microscope to yourself so that you can become a better you. It's hard. It's lonely. It's long.

But it IS the answer. And if you lean into it, you will find the epic life you are searching for, longing for, and wishing for.

So, let's dive in.

Practicing quietude.          Teaching the girls some yoga. 2017

# Chapter 5

The superpower of selfishness is created in baby steps because it is really anti-intuitive. Society teaches us that it is wrong to be selfish and we should pour into everyone else first. Sometimes, I'll even get nasty messages in my DMs about how this message is unhealthy and can hurt people.

What I love about the world is that there is room for all of our opinions. If my message doesn't resonate with you, there are tons of other people to follow and books to read with myriad views on how to develop your life.

Getting selfish is what worked for me. It's what allowed me to flourish in my own way, step into my power, and shine my light on the world.

It didn't feel right at first. Or maybe I just didn't identify it as selfish because that word has such a negative connotation. It's been masquerading as the term "Self-care" because that seems more positive, I guess. But that term isn't deep or meaningful enough to me.

Self-care seems like something you occasionally do to reset or recover.

Selfish is something else entirely. To me, it means a way of living that includes putting yourself first so that you can be the best version of yourself to everyone you love.

Seems like a really positive way to spin it, no? If I think of a better term while I write this, I'll be sure to use it. But so far, my creative juices haven't come up with some magical buzzword that encapsulates the deeper meaning of how this concept totally changed my entire life for the better.

It's hard to fit all that magic into one tiny word.

In contrast, one tiny step can make a big impact, so let's start there.

In quiet comes clarity. And living with two kids full-time without another adult in the house doesn't bring a lot of quiet to your life. Especially when those two kids are two animated daughters who have a zest for life that is contagious and enthusiastic, something I adore about each of them but have a hard time synthesizing first thing in the morning.

I always thought it was cute to wake up with them, especially on the weekends. You see those movies where the family wakes up altogether, all happy and jolly. In trying to be a super mom, I had goals for that picture-perfect family morning.

The thing was, it never felt magical. Because I was adjusting to life as a single parent, still mourning the loss of a marriage, and trying to figure out how to wrangle thirty male barbers at MadMen, I was pretty on edge. The pressure of life was slowly leaking out of me like steam from a pressure cooker.

The girls woke up so excited and joyous, bounding off the walls and talking a mile a minute while my head was swirling like the exorcist with to-do lists for both family and work and a lot of emotions that I was trying to keep under control.

The more I tried to harbor this familial moment in the morning, the more irritated I became. I'd match their enthusiasm with some dark, angry energy that would slowly kill their spirit, and then the mom's guilt and judgment would set in. How could I dull their spark like that? What is wrong with me? Why can't I just be happy?

Despite all I lost, I still had a lot to be thankful for. A beautiful home that I started to redecorate for a new vibe and environment. Two beautiful kids who were slowly healing from an angry divorce. A thriving business. Why couldn't I get my act together and be grateful?

So much judgment. Damn. No wonder I wasn't happy yet. The voice I heard all the time, in my own head, was so negative! Always demeaning my self-worth and putting these unrealistic expectations on my behavior at a time when I was struggling to heal. How can anyone live with such a ruthless witch?

Sound familiar?

The voice you hear the most is your own. It babbles in your head all day and sometimes takes over entirely without you even being aware of the impact.

Awareness leads to control and change.

I started to realize this angry voice wasn't what I wanted to hear all day. This angry voice isn't what I wanted my kids to hear coming out of my mouth.

It was time to change the narrative—literally.

Depression, no matter how slight, makes you lethargic and tired. So I was sleeping until about eight am when my kids would wake me up. I realized that in order to become a nicer person in the morning and more enthusiastic for the girls, I had to wake up before them. I had to give myself some time to have my own thoughts without interruption, organize my day, and maybe even exercise. The thought of waking up before eight did not sound super enticing, given my level of stress and anxiety, which was exhausting. But I had an inkling that this may make me a better parent in the morning, and we all know my goal to be a super mom was a very motivating factor for me.

I started small. I woke up at seven. That gave me a full hour to have coffee and gather my thoughts before the girls jumped out of bed with the force of happiness behind them.

This small change of sixty minutes made a world of difference. I would meet their excitable screams with a huge hug, sometimes even a fun, energized song, and we would have breakfast together, sitting on our countertops, chatting away. They seemed delighted by this new change, and frankly, so was I. Breakfast became a really meaningful time for the three of us to bond and grow closer. All because I woke up earlier and gave myself some "me" time.

Hmmm. Maybe I was on to something here after all.

At first, that extra hour a day was me drinking coffee and trying to manifest normal brain functioning before the kids woke up. But a few months into that, I decided to actually get more intentional with that hour of time. It occurred to me that if I used it with more purpose, I could potentially extend its impact.

This was the start of my morning routine.

One small move has impacted my life for the last seven years. I saw how much waking up earlier, before the kids, turned me into a more present parent, a happier person, and made my day run more smoothly. That impact became addicting, and I wondered how I could utilize it further to increase my productivity and happiness.

Turns out, that was just the beginning of my addiction to tranquility and alone time. I slowly set the alarm clock earlier and earlier. A half hour here and there eventually turned into a four am wakeup. A coffee and some light brain activation turned into a full-on routine of exercise, yoga, meditation, and gratitude.

The more I consistently kept this routine, the more in tune I became with myself. With what I want, with where I want to go, and with how to get there. The more people told me that I seemed happier and more motivated. The more I felt aligned with my real purpose in life.

It was weird witnessing my own transformation like that. At first, I wasn't even aware of what was happening. It just felt right, so I went with it. But eventually, I looked back and saw that the more I stayed committed to this daily morning ritual of selfish time, the happier I had become. I was less anxious, more productive, and felt more excited about each and every day. I woke up ready to slay in life, business, and at home.

My daughters were more excited to spend time with me because I was showing up differently. I was less irritated, had a more positive outlook on things, and was not as quick to yell or blame.

My businesses were flourishing because I was showing up differently. My leadership was more predictable and calm. I was more dedicated to problem-solving than deflection and blame.

My internal happiness was off the charts. My immediately-after-wakeup workout left my mind clear, which was the perfect time to meditate. All the feels would come up in my ten-minute meditation. I would get inklings of exactly where I wanted my day to go, my life, my dreams. So after meditation, I would journal outside because the fresh air made me feel grounded. I'd write about what came up for me during meditation. Sometimes that was despair, anxiety, and fear. Sometimes it was dreams, hope, and desires. And I would say five things I am grateful for. Not just a list of five one-word elements but sentences that got detailed about why it made me happy and brought me joy.

This routine became something I couldn't live without. A staple. A superpower because it gave me the gift of self-awareness and introspection. It taught me how meaningful the stillness was. It got me addicted to the quiet time where I got to analyze who I was and who I wanted to become instead of fearing that conversation with myself.

All because one day, I decided to wake up sixty minutes earlier. All because I decided to selfishly devote the first few hours of my day to ME: the person who holds this family together, the person that leads three companies. The person that raises two kids alone.

With out me, this family can't survive. Without me, businesses can't flourish in the same way. Without me, the girls can't have an amazing life filled with adventure, happiness, and experiences.

If I don't take care of myself, everything else falls apart. And this was the first moment of clarity where I really saw the truth behind the art of using selfish as a superpower.

Chapter 6

My version of selfishness came in a lot of different forms. Most of us wear several different hats each day, and I am no different. So, if we have different parts of self to cultivate, we must also get selfish in more than one way so we can spark a light in each of those lanes.

One important lane for me was finding my footing inside my own business.

Those first few years after my divorce were what I like to call my first come-up. At least at the time, I *thought* that was my come-up story. Turns out, it was only one of many. It was training me to lay the foundation for the next-level stuff I would eventually attempt that, at the moment, seemed pretty out of reach (but... more on that later).

Finding footing inside my own business took a lot of self-discovery. My motivation to provide for the girls and I is what really gave me the courage to go down the scary path of diving into my own insecurities and trying to overcome them. Those momma bear instincts are some powerful emotions. Without them, I probably would have avoided doing the tough work because who wants to go into the deepest darkest places of their soul and poke the feelings that scare you the most?

It isn't a fun exercise. A single-income household with two kids 100% on your own is a big motivator and, in my case, a huge blessing because I dove in head-first and didn't have time to look back or question myself, even for a minute. My family's success depended on my ability to take decisive action and make miracles happen.

If you recall, one thing I struggled with as a working, married mom was getting a babysitter. I felt all kinds of guilt bubbling up to the surface if I had to get a babysitter in my "off" hours.

Well, this divorce really pressed all the emotional buttons and limiting beliefs surrounding this block. Not only did I have to get a babysitter so I could go to work at the barbershops, but I also needed one if I was ever going to leave the house untethered. My kids were four and one. I couldn't leave them alone. They weren't in school. They were home 24/7. There was no reprieve unless I purposefully created one and hired someone to watch them for a few hours.

Hiring a babysitter killed me a little bit inside. I chastised myself for leaving Wall Street to have more time with the girls, only to hire someone to watch them so I could build a business. What kind of mother does that? (Tons). Is it possible to even be a good mom if you're building a career? (Yes!)

When I got to MadMen, I felt so lit up. It made me feel good to find the leader in me and use it to build a company that stood on its own, without ties to the previous lawyer version of myself. But it also felt really awful because the girls wanted me home; I promised them I would be home. But that was before my world was turned upside down. For me, circumstances changed drastically, but to the girls, I was breaking a promise to them.

Heartbreak. Guilt. Pressure.

It all came at me hard and fast. My intuition was telling me to go build out this business and learn how to be a real business-woman. While the mom guilt was pulling at my heartstrings.

If I feel so bad about going out to build the business, why did that success also feel so good? I had to remind myself: Because you are more than a mom!! You're a person too!

Oh, yea! I was a person. I had almost completely forgotten because ever since having kids, all I had identified as was a mom. All everyone saw me as was a mom.

A person. How fascinating. Maybe I should lean into that portion of myself a little more, huh? Let's give it a whirl.

It seemed like a necessary step in my evolution for me to get a little selfish and build a career not only outside of being a lawyer but also outside of being a mom.

So, I hired a sitter for three full days a week. This was a huge compromise for me. Four days mom-ing, three days being Jessica (remember her? I didn't...yet). In those three days, I would work at the shops, run errands and squeeze in some personal time in the form of yoga and crystals.

Tire Screech. Crystals? That came out of left field a little, didn't it...let me explain.

How does Lawyerly Jessica, attorney-slash-business owner by day (well, three days at least) and Super Mom by night, find time to also be part hippy?

Well, I spent those first years post-divorce figuring out how to take care of myself again. The only other time I had really poured into myself was after the doctors told me I couldn't have another baby. So, I decided in this second dark moment to revisit some stuff I tried during that first dark moment. It worked once; why couldn't it work twice?

Yoga, which I formerly despised because it forced me to get quiet, became my most powerful tool to lean into to find ME.

Along with yoga, I started exploring healing stones (aka crystals) again. I found myself at this spiritual store (that the girls and I call the Healing Store) at least once a week, trying to understand what each crystal does and how I can use them to start reminding myself of this power that self-help books claim I have deep inside of me. That was when the rebirth of my Bra-Rocks stage began.

Healing stones became the gateway to the new me. I know that sounds a little weird, but hear me out on this because it's not as much about spirituality as it is about presence, self-talk, and daily reminders, which most of you could use a little more of if we are being honest.

What I learned about crystals is they can be used as a powerful reminder of where I am headed. When I was struggling, this reminder was the encouragement I needed to keep going.

The mind is a really powerful thing that we constantly underestimate. It has the power to make us or break us, but the good news is that power is within our control. The choice is ours.

HOPE is the most positive motivating factor you can feed the mind. One small word but an emotion that is so powerful it can make miracles become a reality. Remember how my pregnancy journey seemed hopeless? Then that tiny carnelian crystal restored my hope that miracles can happen...and so one did happen.

Hope is THAT powerful.

I use my crystals as a reminder of hope. Hope in the process. Faith in the universe. Remember, hope is what helped me get pregnant with my miracle baby, so at this point, it had proven itself a worthy thing to allow into the high-priced real estate of my brain.

This time, in the front of my mind, I was figuring out who I was outside of law and outside of being a mom. The most hopeful way for me to do that was to lean into my business. A business that I had not really run before with a man who was now less than thrilled with the sight of me. Seemed like a big challenge to overcome, but something inside me screamed: THIS IS IT! This is the way to find out who you really are.

I had no clue how working in my barbershops alongside my ex-husband was going to help me figure out who I really was or lead me to some kind of epiphany or greatness. But I decided to throw my healing stone bracelets on, follow my intuition and lean into what the universe presented to me.

At the healing store, I bought a "business success" bracelet, which was shades of brown and green and had a lotus in the middle. A lotus is a flower that grows up and out of the mud and muck into something amazing. Seemed like the perfect metaphor for what I was trying to accomplish. So, I wore that bracelet alongside a bracelet made of green stones that symbolized financial abundance.

Leaving my job on Wall Street was a HUGE leap of faith because I like financial independence. I never thought I'd leave a financially stable and lucrative job to go all in on a forever tied to my husband. It was scary. Then on top of it, getting divorced and having a bad relationship with him at first made me feel even more unsteady about my financial future.

At the time, I didn't have a growth mindset, and I didn't believe that I could really succeed in a business of my own. I mistakenly thought that I would need to work for someone else to be successful because then my mistakes wouldn't make or break the entire foundation of the company.

In short—I was scared and didn't think I was worthy.

So, I wore these bracelets as a reminder that I could come out of the muck and be a beautiful force in the world AND make a lot of money without the safety of a corporate job.

Anytime I felt unsure or doubted that I could do it (and believe me, that was often), I'd look down at those bracelets or touch them to try and regain my mental strength.

They gave me hope. They reminded me that I might not understand the how, but the universe and my own intuition were guiding me toward where I was meant to be. It was an act of blind faith in myself. And it was scary. I couldn't see the bigger picture. How this divorce, a barbershop, and a few bracelets were going to lead me down this road of crazy success and happiness in every single way.

But, I finally had HOPE that all of those amazing energies would find their way to me.

And they did. But not for five long years.

# Part 3

---

# Embracing My New Superpower...then wielding it like a BO$$

# Chapter 7

It took about eighteen months before I found my footing in my own business. First, I had to find the footing within myself.

Like a lot of women, after a divorce, I had to find my new look. It was more about finding my power again, and what's more empowering than taking control of the way you look? Sometimes its easier to change the physical first before we tackle the intangible, emotional side of our transformations.

The problem was a physical transformation in my style was pretty impossible to do when I had no clue who I was. Once again, I just rooted back into who I used to be before kids and then worked on patching that vibe together with who I was currently in the process of becoming.

In other words, I was testing the waters to see what felt right now that I was morphing into someone I hadn't quite met yet.

Before kids, my spirit animal was nineties music artist Avril Lavigne. She was a tough outer shell with a feminine edge, and I always felt connected to that. She somehow struck the balance of being a strong woman without giving away her girly energy. That is what I was trying to accomplish, but it was hard. I came from a man's world again and again. In high school, I was a jock that played multiple varsity sports and had 99% male friends. I went from that to law school and Wall Street, which are both male-dominant. Now, I was running barbershops with male staff and clients.

Society makes us believe that if we embrace our feminine side, it takes away from our strength. What a load of crap.

Unfortunately, at that time, I believed the nonsense society had told me. I was afraid to overly embrace my feminine side because I didn't want to lose face with my staff or the clientele. So, I decided that I would embrace my inner Avril and do some blond hair and heavy eye makeup always loved that and felt right at home with a harsh, heavy eye-liner. But I had never bleached my hair, so that piece was a BIG deal.

This transformation first happened the night of a big MadMen photo shoot. I remember walking into the shop with my new look plus my new outfit (I went with a feminine blazer because I felt comfy as a half lawyer, half nineties rock star LOL). I felt powerful. It was one of those "fake it till you make it scenarios." That phrase is overused, but the essence is true: if we speak things into existence with authority, we can make these notions a reality.

Curating this new look was part of me TRYING to garner up some power. I didn't feel like an amazing leader or parent, or businesswoman yet, but I thought if I spiced up my look, maybe I could start to turn the tide in the direction of confidence.

It worked.

This was the beginning of my emotional transformation, though I didn't know it at the time. My look, my hair, my makeup, and my style would slightly evolve here and there over the next several years. The beautiful thing is my look, and my power became more and more in sync the more I got to really know myself. The more I got selfish and dove into who I am and who I want to become, the more these slight twists and turns in my physical appearance would effortlessly match who I was in that moment of growth.

It became an authentic flow the more I got to know myself, and that is the important message here. As cliché as it may be, "fake it till you make it" has a ring of truth. That first step of trying a new style on for size allowed me to gain some traction in setting out to find ME. It gave me a little boost of energy I needed to garner the courage to take on the world as a newly single mother of two who also wanted to be something more....though I wasn't quite sure what "more" would be just yet.

I wasn't afraid to pivot or try something new as I kept changing. I leaned into what felt right, even if it didn't quite make sense. One day I'd go all out nineties band t-shirt, crimped hair, black jeans, and combat boots. The next day I'd be in a blazer with pin-straight hair and heels. If it felt right, I wore it. I gave myself permission to allow each part of me to shine, even if those parts didn't quite have a cohesive flow yet.

Granting yourself permission is such a huge step in self-development. Yes, society puts these pressures on us to act or dress or live a certain way. But this pressure can only really affect us if we *allow* it to affect us.

That's the thing most women don't understand. You have control. You control which words or expectations affect you words or expectations affect you, your mindset, and your actions. You control where your energy flows, what you focus on, and who you associate with.

These seemingly little things make a big impact. Each person you allow into your space, each thought you allow into your brain is you granting permission for it to affect you. That effect can be negative or positive, but either way, it was allowed by you.

Over the years, what I learned is I can only control myself. And therefore, my happiness and my attitude, and my energy have to come from within me because ME is the only thing I can control. Whenever my happiness came from what other people thought or said or how they acted, everything would fluctuate; my moods, my confidence, and my energy.

Once I learned to have the sun rise and set with ME, I became more emotionally stable, happier, and brighter. Why? Because I can control only one thing in this world: I. And if I take the driver's seat in my own life, I can flip my perspective on everything everyone else does and says. I can decide whether I give it permission to be part of who I am or if I reject it and keep going on my merry way.

THAT is power. And it starts with using selfish as the super-power it is!

The power that I radiated in that MadMen photoshoot wasn't because my hair was blond, or my eye makeup looked insanely good, or my outfit was new.

The power came from owning the room. From taking back my control. From disarming the atmosphere so that whatever the bar-bers or my ex-husband were thinking about me didn't matter, it just all fell away. All that mattered was what I thought of myself.

Something had changed. I showed up, ready to carve my own path and be a driving force in my own life. I didn't know how I would do it or where that path was leading, but I was ready to go take over the world. And everyone in that room felt it.

Grand Opening Party of MadMen's second location, 2016

Photo Cred: Hathsin Photography

## Chapter 8

What do you want?

It's a simple question. But can you answer it with conviction and detail? Most people cannot.

I ask this question at my speaking events. I ask this question to my clients. I ask this question to friends I am trying to help. And I'm almost always met with a resounding quizzical look. That look is followed by an explanation of everything they DO NOT want.

Well, that wasn't the question, now, was it?

You get what you focus on, so if you have everything you don't want in the forefront of your mind, that is all you will be getting. Yet most people concentrate their efforts on seeking out what they do not want so they can reject it. They replay their mistakes in their mind over and over again, so they are certain as to what they want to avoid. But they have no idea what they are seeking.

Five years after I left Wall Street to grow MadMen, I could not answer my own question. I had no idea what I wanted, but I knew that I was not the happiest I could be....and that stung.

Imagine this:

- I had a successful business that we built to basically run it-self. That is the dream. For a business to run without you and make money while you sleep, travel, and parent. And I did that.

- I had a beautiful house that I renovated after the divorce to feel more like ME. The girls and I love it here.
- I had two beautiful, healthy daughters who were thriving and happy and whom I got to travel with often.
- And while I was building an amazing company, I was also able to be a super mom; on the board of the PTA, doing every drop-off and pick-up, planning playdates, going to all activities, etc. No nanny. No husband.

I had an amazing life that I was extremely present for and grateful for. I had a life that most people were striving to achieve. But I knew I wasn't the happiest I could be.

MadMen was running smoothly. Neither of us had to be present at the physical store locations anymore. In fact, my ex-husband moved five hours away and now did all the ads and social media remotely. Our staff was consistent and had been with us for a while. Everyone was in a groove. The shops were well-oiled machines, which was amazing. But I was feeling unfulfilled.

Five years prior, I spent my time and energy figuring out how to be a successful leader in a world I knew nothing about. I took the time to develop myself and learn how to lead a company, and now I was in a rhythm. It made me crave more intellectual stimulation. I wanted to challenge myself to grow and evolve, but I didn't know how. The barbershop was my ex-husband's idea and his passion project. I wanted to feel that passion for work again and had to figure out how exactly to do that.

The problem was I was judging myself, and that got in the way of me figuring out what I wanted.

I felt so guilty that I worked so hard to build a life where I didn't have to go to work every day. This gave me the flexibility to do all the things for my daughters: drop them off at school every day, pick them up at 2:45 pm (which is pretty early in the day if you think about it), do their homework with them, take them to activities and playdates, have dinner together every night, be there to tuck them in at night. No nanny. No babysitter. No help. Just me. And I loved that I could do that while also building a flourishing business.

But the truth was: I wanted more. I wasn't as fulfilled and happy as I could be. Yes, I was spending A LOT of time with the girls. But I found myself getting anxious, easily agitated, and restless. So, the time I was spending with them wasn't as focused and present as it used to be.

I was starting to realize that I was not happy. And that made me judge myself ever so badly.

"How dare you want more!"

"You are so spoiled."

"You already have so much; can't you just be happy?"

The myriad of self-degrading comments flooded my head regularly, which only made matters worse. I knew I wouldn't be able to figure out what I wanted unless I got my head on straight, but I also couldn't pinpoint the source of my unhappiness.

Hadn't I gotten everything I set out to achieve? A thriving business that allowed me to be home almost always so I could raise the girls on my own. That is what I wanted. That is what I had. So why am I feeling uncomfortable and restless?

Turns out, I like to be multi-dimensional. During my marriage, I lost myself in my role as a mom. Being home with the girls so much made me start to feel like that was happening again. I wanted to learn from my mistake and not let the mom roller coaster take the driver's seat of my life again.

Turns out, I also like to be intellectually challenged. Yes, I want to grow a company that doesn't need me every single second. But I also want to feel like I am evolving as a person and not just as a mom. I enjoy an exciting life filled with adventure and growth.

In my "mom life," I was surrounded by married women who were not the breadwinners. This was in stark contrast to me, one of a few single moms at school and the only one (I know of) who was solely financially responsible for the kids. Throw on top of that being a small business owner, and I was basically an alien to the other women around me.

I was active on the board of the PTA, but that didn't light me up. Sitting on the sidelines chatting with the moms at our kid's activities didn't light me up. I didn't want to JUST talk about the kid's schedules, the news, and elementary school parent drama. I wanted to talk about business and wealth building and travel and the struggles I was having as a small business owner. I was also into football, yoga, crystals, and volleyball, and I was dabbling in dating, all of which hardly any other moms could relate to.

At the shop, the customers and staff were all male. There wasn't a ton I could bond with them over. My college friends were all busy with young kids trying to navigate a part of life I was already past.

I was feeling pretty lonely, and the only voice I heard repeating in my head were all the things I didn't want and all the guilt I had from wanting more.

It was a really confusing and lonely time in my life. I didn't know how to fix it because I had never asked myself the question: What do you want?!? I spent my life focusing on what I did not want, what I didn't want to repeat, and what I needed to get done.

I was a passenger. Flowing with life's twists and turns, but not actually taking the wheel and navigating life towards the direction I WANTED.

Most of us do that. We let the circumstances dictate what happens. We make a series of seemingly minor decisions based on circumstance, and before we know it, we look back and see an entire trail of "minor" decisions that completely changed the course of our life. We are already so far into the course before we are consciously aware of it, so now we feel like it's too late to take control, so we just keep going.

What a terrible way to live.

How much more powerful would life be if we actually navigated? How much happier would we be if we took action based on what we wanted rather than what we were handed?

It was time for me to get clear on what I wanted, which made me really uncomfortable because I wasn't quite sure. Luckily for me, the universe was about to hand me the most terrifying and stressful "gift" of all: Clarity... and Covid.

A time of crisis acts as the perfect reason to get selfish without feeling guilty. See, we over-achieving givers need to have a really good reason to put ourselves first. Without this reason, we continue to put other people's needs before our own. We trick ourselves into thinking this is for the good of humanity because... you know... we are THAT important. When really, all this does is make us neglect ourselves and become a hot mess that can't help anyone else.

This pandemic was exactly the excuse I needed to tune everyone and everything out (including those mean guilt-ridden voices in my head and do what I needed to do for ME.

My barbershops were shut down and remained so for five months. I had a choice to either ride it out and let the circumstances dictate how my life panned out. OR, I could take the reins and pop into action.

I chose the latter, mostly because keeping myself busy would prevent me from panicking into insanity.

So I popped into action, not realizing that my next steps would completely change the entire trajectory of my life; not realizing that this moment would define me for years to come; not realizing that in 12 short months, I would be a completely different person with a completely different life.

# Chapter 9

Taking back control of your life is a scary flex. Just because we are making decisions with more purpose doesn't mean we always understand how these decisions will affect us for the rest of our lives.

Many times, in order to take control of our lives, we have to make decisions based on what we want without really knowing HOW we will achieve it. That is scary. That takes faith. That takes hope. And sometimes, faith and hope are difficult to maintain during a moment of chaos.

Remember this: you don't always need to know the how.

If you trust your intuition, the how will eventually reveal itself later...when you are ready to hear it.

Some of my best decisions over the last two years came from my intuition. At the moment, it seemed like pure lunacy.

One of the most glaring examples of this is the words you are currently reading. I am writing this at my desk with one goal in mind: this book will become a New York Times Best Seller.

Mind you, at this very moment—15,000 words into the book (around seventy pages) I haven't even hired a book editor. I also don't have a publisher. But what I have is a dream and some "crazy" energized intuition that this book is what millions of women need to hear in order to get to the next level of their life.

Right now, everyone watching this journey on social media probably thinks I am a little crazy. And they aren't wrong. It takes a little amount of loco to move mountains and take flight. I fully embrace the side of me that likes to take big scary chances on things that seem like a long shot because I believe that to accomplish big things, you need to know why it lights you up, but you don't need to know the how.

So, if you are reading this book and it is on the NYT Best Seller list, and I am currently galivanting around the country on a book tour signing books at a store near you, and you are waiting in some crazy line to meet me, just remember: I started this book with nothing but a laptop and a dream.

One day, I decided this message needed to be heard; I took out a blank Word Doc and started pouring my heart into it. Twenty-one days later, I had a manuscript and still no idea how I would turn that into a real live book. Yet here you are reading it.

Don't forget to always keep dreaming and flowing with what you feel inclined to do, what you're passionate about. THAT is what lights up your energy and makes it stronger. Then, your energy will pull the right opportunities toward you.

This book is only one example of that, but I guess it isn't really a good one because that dream has not actually happened yet happened yet at this very moment. So let me dial it back to an example that actually did turn out the way I intended, even though, when I was dreaming it up, it seemed like the greatest long shot yet.

I wanted to speak on stages across the country to entrepreneurs trying to create more freedom in their life.

At the time, I was mostly identifying as a single mom who also owned some successful barbershops that were now shut down. My income was zero. I wasn't a best-selling author, a mentor to entrepreneurs, or a speaker yet. My Instagram following was a measly 1800, and it was 99%, barbershop owners. The world wasn't even open, let alone allowing people to freely travel to events and gather to listen to someone speak on stage, which made my dream seem like total lunacy.

I went to work anyway. I turned to social media.

At the time, my Facebook page was private, and I only used it to periodically showcase my kids and how cute they were. I maybe post ten times a year, and not even about the full spectrum of my life. I never posted about the barbershops. I never posted about the two-year relationship that I was happy in. I was so closed off to sharing my life, my stories, my hardships, and my successes.

My Instagram page was public, but it was all about MadMen's product line for pomades and beard oils. It had a small following of about 1800 and it was mostly barbershop owners and hair product distributors. It was a boring page that never had any life or energy because I didn't feel that revved up about hair products. I never spoke about business and I didn't even show myself there.

Well, that was all about to change.

As a frustrated small business owner shut down with no income, I became really passionate about keeping up the spirits of other business owners who maybe didn't have the means to live off of their savings as comfortably as I could at that time. I wanted to be a source of light and also a source of help. My legal background helped me navigate the shutdown easier than other people, so I figured I could share that knowledge, plus tips about how I was keeping myself sane as a super-driven person incapable of working in the normal way I was used to.

I turned my social media pages into a page about my journey navigating this weird time in our nation's history...the world's history. It felt right, though I did not know how it would be received. It was something I really enjoyed pouring my heart and soul into, so even if no one watched it, it would still be meaningful to me.

To my surprise, people were intrigued. I started going live on how yoga helped me stay fit and calm, how to get small business loans and ideas for what to do once we were allowed to reopen. This got me invited onto some social media shows, podcasts, and even two television broadcasts. I felt the momentum building, but more importantly, I felt the happiness building. Helping small business owners lit me up. I wasn't sure where this would lead, but I was enjoying the journey, so I leaned it. I leaned in hard.

What I learned about myself during this time was that I was a total control freak. Many of you can relate to that, I'm sure. We think the world should bend to our will and meet our desires when really, the world is turning and shifting with or without us.

This represented a time in my life (and most of our lives) when things were 99% out of my control and could not be wrangled. I learned the important lesson of only trying to control what I could actually control: my emotions, the way I reacted to people and circumstances, the way I structured my day, and the words I said to myself, even in the privacy of my own head (self-talk is such a crazy important thing in your life).

For everything else, I surrendered to the flow of life. What does that mean? In short, when I felt lit up or passionate about something, or I felt like a decision was right for me, I went with it. I leaned into it. Even if I wasn't sure how it would work, fit into my life, or it would be successful. I let life continue around me, gently nudging me here or there and being more flexible and open to hearing what the world was telling me, even if it didn't quite make sense to me.

To many of you, that seems far-fetched. At the time, I felt that same way. The only difference is the circumstances were so powerful at that moment I was kind of forced into allowing myself to surrender. If not for the intense situation at the time, I may have tried to force my way into control. Good thing the universe had other plans for me.

Surrendering to the moment proved to be the most powerful force in all the success that transpired in my life over the last two years.

Let me show you how surrendering got me exactly what I wanted.

Being at the beach helps me surrender.

Outdoor yoga is a powerful tool. 2021

# Chapter 10

It was December 2020, and my life was in a groove. I spent most of the last nine months trying some stuff out for size that didn't quite fit until it did.

It started with Instagram lives, which led to some collaborative ambassador influencer nonsense, which led to being asked on podcasts.

- Pause -

What the heck was a podcast anyway? I had two little girls at home that never stopped talking to me. When I got in my car, I soaked up the silence like it was water in the middle of a desert. The absolute last thing I wanted was to listen to someone else talk at me. I didn't understand why people, in the blissful silence of their car without kids hanging on them and the freedom to do whatever they wanted, would listen to a podcast. But I digress. Whenever someone asked me to be a guest, I said yes. Because....I wanted to help, and it seemed this was the way!

- Un-Pause -

Podcasts led to some minor TV talk show appearances on local networks, which led to some networking that landed me on a call with someone who majorly influenced what is arguably the biggest PIVOT of my life thus far. I go into more depth on this in my first book, *Pivot & Slay,* but for our purposes here, what you need to know is that we met through a mutual friend, and after speaking one time, he encouraged me to write a book about my life and introduced me to a book editor.

That was the birth of *Pivot & Slay:* my book and my motivational speaking/consulting business. Before writing my book, I really had no idea what I was doing. I kept following my intuition, which was telling me to talk about business on social media, be a guest on podcasts, and go on these shows. But to what end?

I didn't close these appearances with a Call to Action. I didn't have a product or service to offer at the end of the appearances. I was just showing up, sharing my knowledge, and exiting. I was having fun but making zero dollars and had no idea how to monetize what I was doing.

Writing my book and seeing my journey on paper, in black and white, really connected the dots for me. I finally saw the value in all the lessons I learned through my own failures and successes. This realization encouraged me to keep telling my story and use my unique experiences to help other people grow their businesses. *Pivot & Slay* was born.

Light Bulb Moment.

All this time, I had just been following my gut, which felt uncomfortable without a plan in place. But all the varying pieces of what I had done throughout the nine months had somehow led me to this very moment, learning to mentor others. Even though I wasn't able to see the magic behind the scenes, the universe was leading me exactly where I needed to be.

Writing that book gave me clarity on what direction I wanted to take in my life. Writing that book gave me confidence because as I wrote the story of my life with all its twists and turns, I realized that I was a total badass that had conquered so much and had so much more to give. Writing that book let me see for myself all the magic everyone else had been seeing in me over the last nine months as I navigated my level-up into the woman I was becoming. I thought it was mundane and regular. All these strangers saw it as thrilling and intoxicating.

This book gave me a newfound confidence in myself, and it came at the perfect time. One month later, in December 2020, I got a call that would turn my world upside down in the best and scariest of ways.

Before the call, it was just a regular Monday here in New York. I had written some pages of my book, went to a yoga class, did some work for MadMen, exercised on the boardwalk at the beach (it was exceptionally nice weather for December), and worked on my new website. But then, someone called and offered me an unexpected chance to change things up.

It was one of those moments where you have to decide if you actually want to change your life in all the ways you've been saying you do. Talk is cheap. You want to level up, but are you willing to take the action necessary to bring that to life? Few people are. Most people let their fear hold them back.

I am not one of those people.

A mastermind event was happening in Dallas with a bunch of very successful entrepreneurs. They met up once a month, and it happened to be that their next meetup was Friday. THIS Friday.

Reminder, it was Monday.

Reminder, I am a single mom of two that proudly did NOT have a nanny or babysitter on hand.

Reminder, I hate asking for help.

Reminder, I do not travel without my kids.

Yet, I kept listening. I didn't interrupt with my objections as he told me that this mastermind was full of millionaire entrepreneurs that were really into helping each other level up. That there would be superstar guest speakers pouring their knowledge into the room, that they would be going out to dinner that night to mingle more, and that the event was free.

My mind was racing.

I had been working all of these past nine months, not really knowing what the heck I was doing. And now, I finally had some direction. As I was getting dialed in, another wrench was thrown at me to juggle.

Admittedly, I didn't really understand what a mastermind was. Networking wasn't really my thing. I hated all the people shoving business cards in my face and trying to pitch me. It didn't feel right, and I hesitated to trust anyone who would try to sell themselves to me so freely. This event sounded different. And something inside of me was urging me to go anyway, even though I didn't know what to expect, even though I wasn't nearly as successful as anyone in that room would be. Even though I felt totally out of place and barely even had my business and book conceptualized.

I didn't commit to the phone call because I don't like to back out of my commitments. I remember sounding enthusiastic and saying I would try to work it out, but even as the words came out of my mouth, I didn't quite believe I could pull it off.

Upstairs in my home, I paced the hardwood floor barefoot, staring at the phone. My mind was racing, so I went outside to let my feet touch the ground, trying to calm myself from this terrifying excitement rising up inside of me, a mixture of adrenaline and fear.

It was a beautiful day in New York for December. The patio was freezing, but the sun was shining. I lay on the ground and looked up at the sky, talking to no one and everyone all at once: WHAT DO I DO?

My heart said, "GOOOOOO!"

My brain said, "Yes, but..."

The mom guilt started rising to the surface. I felt restless and started to pace.

My inner dialogue started to take over like a crazy train (I know you know precisely what I mean!).

"Jessica, come on! There is no possible way you can fly to Texas in two days. That's absurd. The girls will be devastated."

Yet…I went back into the house. I went up the stairs and into the hallway closet to grab my suitcase.

"Jessica…do you really even belong in that room? They are all millionaires light years ahead of you in business. You'll be the least successful person in there."

Yet…I opened the suitcase and laid it on the hardwood floor, open and ready to be filled.

"Jessica, you can't be serious. You don't even have anyone to watch the girls."

Yet…I opened up my phone, searched for a flight on Delta, and booked one. Eeeek!

"Jessica, you've never been to a mastermind. You have no clue what to wear or how to look. Your professional clothes are so dated."

Yet…I started lining up my heels and pulling some outfits out of my closet, hanging each outfit on the door frame so I could figure out a look.

"Jessica, you're so selfish. You already have a successful business. This is just a passion project. You're really going to leave your family for two nights over a passion project?"

Yet….I started to pack my makeup, my curling iron, and my laptop.

Against all my inner dialogue…against all logic…I started getting ready for a trip I didn't commit to yet, to see people I didn't even know, in a place I'd never been.

Against all logic, I booked a flight and hotel without even telling a soul or finding a babysitter for an event happening halfway across the country in two days.

I thought taking this trip would be inconvenient for my parents.

It would be devastating to the girls who I had not once left since the divorce.

It would be difficult for everyone because the girls both had school, homework, and activities that I would miss and that they'd have to be chauffeured around for.

Within an hour of the phone call invitation, I had packed a carry-on, booked a flight, and gotten a hotel. I sat on my bedroom floor next to my suitcase, thinking what a lunatic I had become.

Me laying on my floor packing for a trip that changed my life. 2020

# Chapter 11

After my mania died down, I looked around the room.

In two hours, I had to pick up the girls from school, but right now, I was just lying on the hardwood of my hallway floor, looking up at the ceiling. It felt a little bit like waking up in a hangover haze. My mind was racing, trying to make sense of everything that had just transpired as I looked around the room, sorting out the facts. Did everything I remember actually happen? Seems crazy and uncharacteristic for me.

I looked around the room.

Suitcase full of clothes.
Phone opened up to the Delta App.
Pairs of heels displayed on the floor.
Outfits on hangers hanging from the door.

Who am I?
Clearly, my intuition was taking me to a place I had never been before. A world where for once, everything is about to revolve around me; what I want, what I need to be happy. A world where I put myself first. And that was pretty terrifying.

All of the exhilaration of the moment seemed to be sucked out of me. The high I was feeling as I was packing for this new adventure gave way to logical notions of dread, anxiety, and a litany of self-limiting beliefs flooded my brain and replaced all of the heart-felt, excited emotion I had been experiencing.

I was convinced that the universe inside of my home could not run smoothly without me. That the girls would be devastated that I left them for two measly nights to work. That my parents would never agree to watch them overnight because it would be too much, too difficult, and too imposing. That my absence for two nights would somehow negatively impact the barbershops because the barbers would think I was abandoning them or not focused on the growth of the shop.

Really, I was making excuses. Excuses to stay inside the safety of my comfort zone. Excuses to make me think that I had no other choice but to stay, so it really wasn't my decision to remain stagnant…it was my duty for the benefit of others (which makes the "choice" seem selfless and therefore acceptable).

What I realized much later is that this was my fear of expansion rearing its ugly head. I was terrified to change my life because then I had to change my life. I was afraid to up level because I wasn't completely sure what I was doing, how I would do it, or what direction I wanted to go. I was afraid to be around people smarter and more successful than me because I didn't want them to know that I felt inferior. I was afraid that my ex-husband, my parents, and my staff would think my dreams were too far-fetched and impossible for me to achieve, and if they couldn't believe in me, then how could I believe in myself?

This is a problem every entrepreneur faces. It's the reason people get analysis paralysis instead of taking action. They aren't scared of failure. They are scared of success. They are scared of what it will mean to be successful. They are scared of what they'll have to change or let go of in order to become who they really want to be. They're afraid to let go of the things that make them comfortable and grab on to all the things that scare them the most.

They're afraid to soar because they aren't ready to leave the past behind them.

And I was no different. Something inside me was craving this change. Craving this new adventure into the unknown. I didn't even really know what was in store or how this would benefit my life or my business. The HOW was so unclear, but my intuition was screaming YES! It was such a powerful YES that I decided, for the first time in a long time, to ignore my logical brain telling me that I CAN'T and listen to the crazy inner emotional side of me that was screaming at the loudest volume—YES YOU CAN, AND YOU WILL, JUST GO!

It took every single bit of willpower in me to trust myself blindly. The lawyer in me was searching for the evidence: what would the new opportunity bring; let's weigh that against the risk of leaving the girls and asking my parents for favors. But there was no evidence to be had. This was a decision based on emotion alone. On intuition.

When you are faced with such a moment (and if it hasn't come, it will), I challenge you to put your lawyer hat on and look at the evidence of your life. You've come so far—how?

You did not always know the outcome of every possible decision in your lifetime. Somewhere along the way, you made a choice based on how you felt in the moment, even when it didn't seem to make much sense. How did that pan out?

If the choice is a good one, then you can trust yourself to keep leading the way based on your intuition. If that choice didn't pan out, guess what? It still pushed you in a direction towards a lesson of growth.

If you choose to view every decision as a lesson or a win, it becomes a lot easier to follow your heart. There is no negative outcome when we get selfishly devoted to making the choices that light us up at the moment.

So back to the story...

Clearly, I had already made up my mind that I was going. I mean, I booked the flight, got a hotel, and packed the suitcase. But I still hadn't told a soul because I wasn't ready to trust myself. I needed validation from an outside source.

At the time, I had been dating someone for a few years. By now, he was accustomed to my particular brand of crazy when it came to business and following my gut. He knew I was not risk-averse, but he also deeply understood my connection to the girls and my endless desire to be the best parent I could be. He never judged me for that, either. Actually, he always said the kindest things about my devotion to the girls and tried to mimic that with them in every way during our relationship. I knew he was the one person who would understand my turmoil about leaving the girls to do something selfish, so I called him.

This was the first he had ever heard of the Texas trip. I'm sure it took him off guard, and part of him was probably thinking I was crazy, but he handled it with such grace, empathy, and support. He unequivocally and immediately encouraged me to go.

It was a selfless act on his part. We were not in the best place in our relationship. During the shutdown, I had to really dial into myself in order to figure out what I wanted, navigate my businesses, and change the trajectory of my career. I also got really consumed with trying to figure out my new business venture, which was a roller coaster.

He watched as I morphed from running MadMen into a legal Instagram guru, into an advanced yoga instructor, into a brand ambassador, into an author, and more in between. It was a confusing time for me when I was trying to find my new self, and I left him in the dust emotionally.

But at this moment on the phone, he put that all aside to throw his support behind my lunacy and give me the external validation I needed to give me the courage to fly to Texas on a whim one Thursday evening in December.

# Chapter 12

That "selfish" decision changed the trajectory of my life forever in every way.

One upsetting way was that it put a huge strain on what was previously a happy relationship with my boyfriend at the time. At the moment, I felt like my back was up against a wall financially, and I was at a crossroads where I could go explore this new path, or I could stay still and accept what I had.

Staying still had a lot of benefits. I was in love. I had two amazing kids, a house I loved, a business that ran itself (even though it was in rebound mode in 2020 like all other businesses), and I was pretty comfortable financially. To some, I seemingly had it all. And I was extremely grateful for every single element.

But something inside of me wanted more. It felt incredibly selfish...wrong even. I had more than most people, but I knew I could be happier in one aspect of my life: purpose, which really came down to my career. My career felt blah.

MadMen was a huge success, and we were coming up on our ten-year anniversary. I was proud of that. So proud. I had learned so much. Opened three separate shops and got better each time. One was even international, which was a huge learning experience. I had been on billboards in the Dominican Republic, in the news, featured in magazines, and had notoriety on a local level.

But that all felt routine now. I missed that feeling of uncertainty as you build a company striving for success. I missed the exhilaration of learning something new, pushing myself mentally, and having a passion that lit me up.

That fire was missing from me as I went through the routine of my life. I loved spending time with the girls, don't get me wrong. I was excited to be there for every morning, every drop-off, every pick-up, every elongated story about the tiniest thing that happened in each of their days. I was excited to share my day with my partner, go on dates, and cook a family dinner on Sundays. But where I struggled was internally. I needed to feel challenged, driven, and excited about my career too.

I had to choose myself. Something inside of me knew that I had to press pause on everything and chase this little bit of excitement I was getting from starting to build a company from scratch again.

I'm not sure if my boyfriend really understood, but I know that he tried to. And he supported me blindly even though it didn't serve him; it wasn't what he wanted. I am forever grateful that he selflessly encouraged me to go to Texas. Even though everything changed, I wouldn't change a thing. And I know he wouldn't either. We learned some hard lessons about what change and growth really mean. It means you can no longer be the person you used to be. It means you can no longer have what you used to have. You have to make some really tough decisions and let go of some stuff you really, really love in order to grow.

In the end, we let go of each other. And that sucked, not just for us, but for our four children who spent some formative years growing up together, starting at three, four, five and six-years-old. But we let go without judgment or anger. We let go so we could both grow and evolve into who we were meant to become.

In hindsight, this decision was what made us better people. We both faced a lot of things we were avoiding, which made us stronger and happier in the end. But before you get to the good stuff, you have to embrace the suck.

No one warns you about the SUCK.

They tell you to wish for more. Reach for the stars. Dream big. But they don't tell you that in order to do that, you have to let go of some stuff you really love. Some people you really love. Some parts of your life that made you insanely happy at one point.

You can't create your new life if you're stuck in your old life. No one talks about that part. Because it sucks. You're shedding that outer shell that protected you and held you close for so long but doesn't quite fit anymore. And letting it go means this crazy moment of vulnerability…where your new shell hasn't quite grown all the way, which leaves you exposed: to the emotions, to the scary possibility of failure, of loneliness, regret even.

No one talks about that part. Even if you think letting go is the right thing right now, it will still hurt when you close that Chapter for good. You'll probably feel the emptiest you've felt in a while. You'll probably sob more often than you want to admit. You'll probably feel alone, afraid, and worried.

But you have to keep going because that emptiness is the room you need to make for all the light you have wished for, all the happiness, and all the joy.

It IS coming. It's just not immediate. You have to wait around in the suck for just a little bit before that big, beautiful door opens up right into the future you've been dreaming of.

I know because it is exactly what happened to me. And it all started when I flew to Texas for an event I didn't understand with people I didn't know in a place I'd never been.

# Chapter 13

Flying to Texas that Thursday was a decision I made solely based on instinct, without any factual rhyme or reason. If you don't know what that feels like, the best way I can describe it is that something was calling to me from inside my soul. Sounds a little crazy, I'll admit. And I'm ok with that because I live in my truth comfortably, even if that makes you uncomfortable.

Wheels down back in New York, I am feeling totally invigorated and energized from my trip to Dallas. That trip led to an opportunity to fly to Texas monthly to develop myself and my business.

Every month. I knew in my heart of hearts I wanted to jump at that chance, but I had to button up things at home before I could commit to flying halfway across the country once a month.

That was a big commitment. A family huddle was in order because (again) that little voice inside me was nudging me to take the leap and I was fully committed to following it...again.

We went back to the scene of the crime: the upstairs hallway.

- Press Pause -

We rarely do things like other "normal" families. For example, we usually eat dinner sitting on the countertop in my kitchen. If you ask me why, I really can't answer. One day we just did that way and then we didn't stop. All three of our love languages are quality time.

And somehow, on this countertop, we feel connected and present, so now that's what we do.

Unlike most families, we don't stop living just to eat. We eat to live.

We also don't wear shoes a lot. We sit on the floor often. We have dance parties before school. We wake up to happy music. We laugh a lot. We sing even when we don't know the words. And we skip down the boardwalk at our fav beach, screaming out lyrics while people smile, wishing they had the freedom and courage to be themselves.

- Un-Pause -

I tell you all this to say I don't take this family huddle lightly. These girls are the highlight of life. They trust every word I say, even if they don't quite understand what I mean. They watch my actions and mimic them without being consciously aware.

But I see it. I see the way they model themselves after me, not knowing who else to turn to or trust to understand the world around them. And that is a responsibility that I take super seriously.

It's not that I allow the girls to make decisions for our family at such a young age. Clearly, they are not equipped for that, and even if they were, it is too much pressure for a kid.

Instead, I give them a voice, a chance to be heard without judgment or fear that I will be angry. I give them an opportunity to have autonomy so that they see their actions, thoughts, and words can sway the universe. I pride myself on this because it has brought the three of us closer than ever before. We have meaningful dialogue so that the girls can get an explanation of my actions, my words, and my decisions. This is not the way most people parent, and I know that. But I am not most people. I am me, and I am going to make sure my daughters feel heard and supported even if the average parent doesn't believe children have a place around the decision-making table.

So, I called a family huddle when I got back from Texas.

When I got home from the trip, I put my suitcase back in the upstairs hallway and started to unpack (I'm one of those crazy people that unpack as soon as they get home because I hate clutter. Cluttered house = Cluttered mind). My stuff was kind of in flux, but so was my mind, so I decided to let the girls subliminally see where I was at.

We had our family huddle sitting on the floor in the upstairs hallway next to my half-unpacked suitcase.

I was full of energy, and they felt it. They asked me how Texas was, and I told them how much I felt lit up; how it gave me ideas on how to pivot my business and really launch it into space. I told them about how I met some incredible people who had accomplished many of the things I was looking to accomplish. They had big smiles on their faces so far and were listening intently as they felt all my good energy fill the room, the house, and their little souls.

Then I hit the hard part.

See, when I don't know something, I have no problem admitting that. And my convos with my kids reflect that too. So, I got really raw and honest...and told them a little something like this:

I don't know why this is important. I don't know how this is going to help me grow *Pivot & Slay*. I don't know why I need to be in this room every month. But something deep inside of me is telling me to do this. Something is telling me that this is the key to our future; the thing that is going to make us more money and give us more freedom to be together, travel the world, adventure more, and live a more amazing life that will be fun and exciting, and meaningful. And so, even though I don't understand why or how I want to do this.

This would be a big sacrifice for our family, so I want to know how YOU feel. I would be gone two or three nights a month, and you'd have to be with Nana and Papa. I know it is scary. I am scared too. But I want to give you the best life I can. I want to be the most present, best mommy ever. And somehow, I feel like this will be the way.

They both looked up at me, blinking. They weren't totally sure what the heck I was what I was talking about, but they were 100% certain they didn't want me to travel for three days a month.

They didn't say anything at first. Their eyes were getting a little watery. And the anticipation of their thoughts was slowly killing me.

Quinn looked at Emma, as she usually does, for guidance from her big sis on how to feel. She has her own set of emotions and a strong will but didn't yet confidently project her feelings without knowing everyone else's (we've worked on that a lot through the last year...more to come on that).

Emma felt the significance of her thoughts. She knew that whatever she said next was going to mean something. And I saw her carefully contemplating her emotions before she spoke.

She looked me deadpan in the eye. Took a deep breath. And did the most selfless thing any eight-year-old could muster.

She hugged me tight and said, "Mommy, we know you can do it. We are going to miss you, but we are cheering you on."

My eyes welled up because, at that moment, I knew she was being brave and mimicking the way that I parent her. She was trying to muster the courage to support me with the same enthusiasm and encouragement I always show to them. She leaned into her overwhelming trust for me, and even though she only half believed the words she was saying, she went all in on the notion that she knew I could do whatever I set out to do.

Seeing myself through her eyes was all I needed to dig in my heels and make miracles happen. I refused to let down the two people in the world I loved the most, who were putting all their trust and confidence in my ambition.

I squeezed them both so tight with tears in my eyes on the floor of our hallway and kissed the top of their heads, thanking them so much for believing in me and giving me the opportunity to soar. Nuzzled into them, I said, *"I don't know how (yet), but I promise I am going to change our lives in the most incredible way."*

And THAT, my friends, is how you take your family (and even your staff) on the journey with you.

You include them in your decision-making process, give them a voice, and show them that you want them to win too. And the most important thing you can do, as someone once said to me: "Make your dreams so big that everyone else's dreams fit inside of yours."

Eighteen months later, my girls would be sitting in a crowded event space with nearly 300 women in attendance, watching me up on stage as I recant this exact story in all of its suspense and glory with tears in my eyes.

Except this time, at the end of the story, I looked right at them in the audience and said, *"See girls…I told you I would change our lives!"*

All because I packed my suitcase. The speech I gave with my daughters
in the audience. Dallas, 2022

Photo Cred: 7 Seconds Media

The girls & I after my speech
in Dallas. 2022

Photo Cred: 7 Seconds Media

# Part 4

---

# Elevate beyond the Hustle

# Chapter 14

What happened in the eighteen months between those two convos with my daughters is where all the magic lies.

Some of you are home right now, thinking, man, next year is so far away to think about. You think you have all the time in the world to start starting.

Some of you are home right now thinking one year is too close; it isn't enough time to change your life. It's too fast; it will come so quickly, and you can't make a lot of movement in the next twelve months.

Both of you are right. And both of you are also dead wrong. It is far away, but it is also so close. You have all the time, yet not enough time.

Instead of lecturing you on what you could be doing, let me tell you a bit about how my life completely changed in just over one year.

Rewind to the beginning of this story, circa 2019, when I was an unenthusiastic, underwhelmed barbershop owner...

At the heart of it, I was seemingly living the dream. The barbershops had been thriving for eight full years. Through trial and error that mostly involved following our gut instincts, we navigated myriad problems along the way; staffing issues, customer complaints, people attempting to steal our branding and ideas, divorce, international business ownership in the Dominican Republic, and so much more.

Somehow, someway we were able to instinctually pluck ourselves out of the ground level of the business over those eight years. Where we used to sweep the floors, run the register and serve coffee, at some point, we recognized that our worth to the company far exceeded any of those more menial tasks.

The realization came to me one day as I was sweeping in between barber chairs. It was kind of therapeutic, and I was in deep thought. My mind was racing with all of the things I had to get done behind the scenes for the shops to thrive. At that time, we had two shops in New York and one overseas in the Dominican Republic. There was so much to do on the back end of the business. It made me realize: why am I here sweeping the floor when I can be home making big money moves for the company?

My purpose for the company was so much greater than my presence at the shops. I had big things to accomplish and high-level tasks to conquer. My focus had to be elsewhere, and I had to take the leap to stay home and do the things that would make the business thrive.

So many business owners are scared to let go at that point. They don't want to relinquish control of the small stuff because they feel like no one can do it as well as they can. They don't want to give up their presence at the business because they don't trust the staff to work well without them. They feel like staying in their lane would somehow inhibit the business from growth, when really it is the thing the business needs the most to take off to a new level.

I dive into this part of my journey in great detail in my first book: *Pivot & Slay*. So, for now, I'll just say that at the end of 2019 and the beginning of 2020, I found myself a little lost. I had gotten really clear on what my role was at MadMen and was totally focused on just that narrow lane of expertise.

All that focus freed up space in my head and in my day that I didn't know how to utilize. I spent the last three years singularly focused on MadMen's growth and my growth as a leader. I had accomplished so much in that regard, and now I found myself butting up to that comfort zone I hated so much.

I don't know about you, but I experience this every few years. I have my sights set on my big scary goals, and as I start to check them off my list and conquer them one by one, I realize I need more of that excitement and challenge to drive me. It happened in my legal career when I hit a wall in my development as an attorney and outgrew the New York Stock Exchange. And it happened again at MadMen when I felt like I had learned all I could in running that company, and I needed something to challenge me to get to the next level.

The problem was I wasn't quite sure what I needed. My intuition was screaming: THIS ISN'T ENOUGH! Ok, great. Message received. But what would be enough? Would anything ever be enough? What else could I even dream of accomplishing?

These questions boggled my mind as I tried to figure out what the heck I even wanted.

Have you ever stopped to ask yourself that question: What do you want? It seems like a pretty straightforward question, but it is actually one of the most difficult questions to answer.

In 2020, I couldn't answer that simple question. In hindsight, I know it was because I lost myself. I lost myself in the roles I played: Attorney, then Wife, then Mom, then Business Owner.

What about Jessica, the person? The human was at the core of all the roles I was playing.

I was always doing doing doing. Taking action after action without having my larger purpose in my sights. I was waking up, doing all of the things I had to do to fill the roles, but I was not fulfilling Jessica. Remember her?

Before all the roles, I was a person. A human. Right now, I am a human DOING. I had to get back to a human BEING.

You can run a thriving business without taking care of YOU. You can surely hit six figures, too, without taking care of yourself and without doing any self-development at all. The six-figure mark is one that involves strategies, risk-taking, and grit.

But if you want to go beyond that six-figure mark…if you really want to get to the next level not just in gross revenue but in business development, you've got to get focused on YOU. You have to get selfishly devoted to your happiness, your inner peace, your consistency, discipline, and passion.

Without YOU at your best, your company will forever coast at six figures. You cannot get beyond that without turning inward and getting clear on why you get up every day to grind and where you want to take your life, your family, and your company.

This next level requires a different version of you. A more emotionally intelligent version. A more selfish version. A version of you that understands what you need, what you want, what makes you happy, and then goes out to grab all of that high vibe energy to bring back to your family, your staff, and your brand.

That higher vibrational energy is the inner work that no one else is willing to do. It's that scary, introspective awareness that everyone else is afraid to put under the microscope. It's the energy that sets entrepreneurial legends apart from the average small business owner.

To get to the next level, you have to level up yourself from the inside out.

It's the moment where we see how badly you really want all the things you say you do.

# Chapter 15

In 2021, *Pivot & Slay* hit six figures in gross sales. It took me twelve months to hit that mark, and I exceeded my financial target by a lot.

That is pretty impressive, even if I do say so myself. Multiple six figures in twelve months, from inception to year-end, with no staff.

I told you—you can hit six figures with no problem. The only thing that requires is hustle.

Hustle and grit also got me a bunch of other accolades, including several features in top-tier business magazines like Forbes, Entrepreneur, Inc, LA Weekly, and many, many more. The hustle built my following significantly on Instagram and started to give me momentum on Facebook. The hustle got my book to hit bestseller on the day it was released. The hustle got me recognized as a top-tier business consultant, which led to other opportunities in organizations far bigger than *Pivot & Slay*. The hustle landed me on private jets, inside rooms of entrepreneurs with far greater knowledge and net worth than me, quoted in other people's books, and on over fifty podcasts. The hustle helped me land my first speaking engagement in December 2021.

The hustle can get you far. It can make you money. It can feel super rewarding.

That is why most entrepreneurs stay there for years and years. The hustle is completely built on business strategy and your willingness to put in the long hours and time to do the ground floor work.

Entrepreneurs stay there not because it is easy but because it is EASIER than taking that deeper dive into themselves. It is easier to stay busy than sit in the quiet, contemplating the tough questions that elevate your life: what do I want? How can I improve; what does success really mean to me; how do I define freedom and happiness; how can I have it all?

Those questions are much more difficult questions to ask, and they are the ones that will take your life to the next level. But it ain't easy. It's arguably more difficult than burning yourself out in the grind every day for fourteen hours. It's harder than handing over your last $5k to start up your crazy business idea. It's harder than taking all your money and throwing it on black.

Sitting in the quiet thinking about who you are and how you can improve means you have to get honest with yourself. You have to hit a new level of communication with yourself. You have to start needling those past storylines and limitations that hurt to think about.

A lot of people dream about success, create goals, and talk a big game about how much they want to take over the world, but few people actually execute. That's because they are not willing to get honest with themselves.

At the end of 2021, I exceeded my revenue goals and hit every moving target I set out to achieve that year. My 2021 goal board was filled with crazy big (mostly financial) goals I thought were impossible at the start of the year, yet I literally annihilated each one by the end of the third quarter—three months ahead of schedule.

I knew it was time to dream bigger. It was time for some next-level ISH. It was time to get dialed into the deeper level of who I am and what I want. It was time for me to get brutally honest with myself. To look at the environment around me and decide what the hell I wanted and if I was willing to make the changes inside of me that were necessary to get what I said I wanted.

2022 was the year everything would elevate at rapid speed, and my life would take an amazing turn in an unexpected direction.

Me walking onto the biggest stage of my life (so far). 2022

Photo Cred: The Brand Digital Media

# Chapter 16

Instead of committing my goal board to achievements centered around money and targets, I created an entire 2022 Dream Board centered around my happiness.

How selfish is that?? An entire year's worth of goals, all centering around the things that make me insanely happy and fortify my high-vibe energy. The things that light me up.

It felt uncomfortable. Really uncomfortable, actually.

My goals would normally be ones that include everyone and everything I care about—all the businesses, both the girls, a little of myself, and 100000% my finances. But this time, I was zoomed in on myself.

2021 had been the year of the hustle. I buckled down to do the work every single day at four am. My head was down, grinding, and I gave up my social life. My free time was to be with the girls and nothing else. It was work and mom mode only, and this was by design. I knew that this was what I needed to kick-start my business.

The hustle is that masculine energy inside of each of us. That drive, ambition, and fortitude, we need to take action and make money moves that can change our world.

Now I was looking to grow not just a business but an empire. And to build an empire, you have to build up yourself first.

I say that as if it is obvious, but believe me, it was not obvious to me. I thought the hustle was THE thing. I thought the grind would get me to new heights. But by the end of 2021, I was shot. I was burnt out and tired and had given every ounce of energy I could to *Pivot & Slay*, but it stopped growing. No matter how hard I pushed, I couldn't get it to the next level.

Why? I lacked vision.

Crafting a vision takes more emotion, insight, and awareness. That takes tapping into your quiet, introspective feminine energy so you can become more in tune with what you need, where you are lacking, and how you can make those small changes that make a big difference.

When you're on the ground floor so frequently—day in and day out—you don't make time to THINK. You don't make time to DREAM because you are too busy doing.

That was me. I had my nose to the grindstone but then hit a wall while I wasn't looking.

It was time to look up to the sky. To connect to the higher version of me that would allow myself to dream and create a larger vision for my life, my business, and my family. It was the opposite of grounding. I had to let myself float up to the stars and see the infinite possibilities before me. (It may sound a little out there but don't worry. I'll come back down to earth and give you some strategies to work with here!)

The only way to do that was to get selfishly devoted to my own happiness.

It was time to think and dream and immerse myself in the energy within me. I knew connecting to myself again was going to be the key to me bringing *Pivot & Slay* to a new level. Prioritizing myself would allow me the space to grow into the powerhouse motivational speaker, author, and business women I knew I could be. But to garner that kind of influence and notoriety, I had to really dive deep into ME. I had to harness all of my energy to create a movement that was larger than life.

In order to do that, to tap into the hearts of other people, and to help them move their life in an insanely successful direction, I had to first do that for myself.

Speaking on stage was something I had grown to love. I first stepped on stage in December 2021, and it was thrilling. I was nervous as hell. I had spoken in front of groups of people before, in court and even as a mentor, but mostly at the head of a conference room, never on a stage. Stepping up to a platform and looking out over a crowd was a different kind of feeling.

Before I stepped on that stage, a mentor said to me: Remember, you belong there. Say that to yourself before you get on any stage. And don't forget—they won't remember what you say; they'll remember how you make them feel.

Feel.

It was all about the feelings.

Having an amazing stage presence starts with being able to get the audience to feel things, to connect to you, but more importantly, to connect to themselves. Say something about your journey that makes them see a little of themselves inside your story and your energy. That is what makes a great connection; that is what impacts lives; that is what sets a great speaker apart from a mediocre one.

And feelings were precisely what I was lacking.

I got on that stage in December 2021, and I knew right away that it lacked passion. I could feel it while I was standing up there. I even remember, at one point, coming out of the zone and making eye contact with someone in the crowd. They looked really enthusiastic (and later even became a consulting client), but at the moment, I felt like I could be giving more. I felt like my enthusiasm should have been higher, my passion more intoxicating.

That day I said everything I planned to say, and I taught everything I intended to teach, but my emotions were lacking. I had spent 2021 inside the hustle and strategy on the ground floor of my business, and I wasn't in touch with my higher purpose inside or outside the business.

Yes, I wanted to be successful, but success without purpose is not fulfilling. To be really fulfilled, you must connect that success to a higher intention. You must have a reason why that success is important. Hitting eight figures, for example, can be the goal. But if you don't know why you want that money and what the money would mean to you on a deeper level, hitting that goal will never bring you the happiness you are searching for.

Stepping off that stage, I knew that if I wanted to be a better speaker and if I wanted to reach my audience in a more meaningful way, I needed to step inside my own heart and feel the feels. I needed to spend 2022 working on a higher connection to myself, so I could infuse that energy and passion into my messaging, create a more impactful connection with the audience and really establish my personal brand and authority in the business world.

It started out as a business goal: connect to myself so I can connect to my audience. But what I've realized since is that taking these steps to get selfishly devoted to my own happiness not only changed the course of my business and added to its success, but it also changed the course of my connection to myself, my children, my family, and the people that I love.

But it all started with me.

Like many entrepreneurs, feelings aren't something I was totally comfortable embracing. Until I stepped on that stage and fell flat, I was resistant to leaning into my emotions. I wanted to stay in the masculine energy of doing, pushing, and achieving. I didn't want to get derailed by emotion because that would take me out of the zone and make me feel things that I didn't have time to feel.

Sound familiar?

The thing is, feelings WILL derail you a little bit.

You may have to hit pause on your financial goals and your business development goals for a hot second so you can actually process the emotion in a meaningful way and use it to grow. Think of this as a slingshot moment. You pull back the slingshot right before you launch it into orbit. That pullback is the moment in time where you pause and lean into the feelings.

That pullback is the moment where you choose you and your own enlightenment because you know leaning into your emotional maturity will help you infuse your own unique and intoxicating energy into your life.

You don't have to listen to me. You can stay where you are doing what you're doing, coasting around the same level you've been stuck at just so you can avoid feeling anything deeper.

But if you really want the success and happiness you claim you want, the key is to stop avoiding the emotion behind it all. Without emotion, success falls flat. You can hit all your targets and still not feel an ounce of pride, happiness, or fulfillment. If you don't feel those things, why are you working so hard??

Get in touch with the passion behind the numbers. Get in touch with the human behind the company. Get in touch with the deeper meaning of why you wake up every single day pushing yourself to the limit. And create goals with the intention of fanning the flame of that passion trapped deep inside of you.

# Chapter 17

My 2022 goals reflected this mindset and were all about my happiness and my fulfillment.

Don't misunderstand. I had some financial and business goals written down as well. But the board was not all about strategy and achievements. It was half (or maybe more than half) about personal enlightenment. And I knew that would lead to the finances because how could it not? If I am lit up and passionate and focused, the money will follow.

I started with these personal goals:

- Two-hours of uninterrupted "me time" every single morning without my phone
- One-hour workouts seven days a week
- Two live yoga classes every week
- Six one-on-one dates a year with each of my daughters
- Spend two nights out with my friends every month
- Get one massage or facial per month
- Take three big trips and two small trips with the girls (Iceland, Utah, and Disney were our big trips. A snowboarding trip and Texas for that women's event I spoke at were our small trips)
- Travel to two brand new places I've never been

- Attract a serious, healthy romantic relationship that fits the criteria of my ideal spouse

This goal list elevated my life.
It elevated my happiness.
It elevated my family dynamic.
It elevated my businesses.
It elevated my income.

All because I finally realized that being selfish was actually a super-power tool I could use to elevate not only myself but my family, my income, and my happiness.

This goal list was the first step I took to getting recommitted to my own emotional intelligence and growth. And because the results were so immediate and so impactful, the list quickly took on a life of its own, evolving into a new routine of daily tasks that fuel my soul and light my passion on fire.

If you follow me on social media, you already know some of the ways I invest in myself every day. But for those of you who don't follow me yet (..sheesh, I mean, head over to your preferred platform already and find me @thejessicadennehy), here is a little flavor of how my goal list morphed into a daily routine I cannot live without.

**Free Resource Alert**: Head over to the free *Pivot & Slay* book resources on my website, jessicadennehy.com, to download my daily routine and learn how to create one for yourself.

My commitment to daily workouts, yoga twice a week, a facial or massage every month, and two hours of me time every morning gave me space to THINK. During this time, I was disconnected from the world, from technology, and from distractions. I was focused and calm, and my mind was quiet. This made space for me to have a more creative flow of energy. More ideas, more dreams, and more visions came to life during this "me" time. It also gave me clarity on each thought passing through my brain, rather than just allowing all the mind chatter to take over. My awareness of each thought, each fear, and each discomfort was clear and acknowledged, allowing me to more fully recognize what areas of my life needed more organization, more attention, or more TLC.

At the same time, these same activities helped me elevate my physical appearance. I started to see my muscles become more defined, my skin clearer and more youthful, my energy heightened, and muscle fatigue diminished. I started to take more risks in my workout, pushing myself to try things I used to think were impossible such as pull-ups. The mental clarity I achieved through these activities gave me the courage to try something new and challenge myself.

Because these physical commitments to myself made me feel so grounded and clear, I started to explore ways to feed my quest for more mental agility and awareness. The year prior, I was reading books that fed my ambition and my need for that adrenaline rush to keep me on target for my business goals. But this time around, I was seeking out books that would feed more of my soul and a quest for knowledge that touched more on the exploration of me as a person and how to find my inner peace, whatever that meant for me.

This quest became addicting in the best ways. I read books that, in previous years, I would have described as "too hippy" or too "woo woo." Ever used those terms? Congrats, you are denying yourself your feminine energy. You are denying yourself the ability to dream bigger by avoiding the emotion and feelings that come with your feminine side.

This isn't just for the ladies, either. Men, if you're reading this, guess what? You have a feminine side too. We all have both energies. The masculine energy represents our ambition, our action, and our ability to compete with others, win and show how amazing we are. A great way to mentally depict this energy is by describing it as the sun because it is vibrant, energetic, powerful, and knows how to bring the heat!

The feminine energy is equally important, but more like the silent strength of the moon. It is calm, cool, and collective. It isn't an outward, boisterous force like the sun. It isn't as intrusive and in-your-face. Instead, it's that introspective energy that comes out in the silence but is still forceful. It can envelop you like the dark night, but it is meant to turn you inward. To get you up in your feels so you can dream bigger.

Imagine the dark night sky. Not even at night, but early morning. Like 3 a.m. The world is asleep. You creep outside in the night time and lie on the ground. The sky is lit up by the moon and the stars, and even though that light is powerful enough to cut through the darkness, it still feels very subtle. And as you lay under the stars, you feel small in comparison to the night sky. You start to think about how endless and massive the universe is; how much possibility there is.

Even though this energy is quiet and gentle, it still impacts you; it makes you feel expansive, like anything is possible, while also making you feel like the ripple you have is so small in comparison that taking a shot cannot possibly have the catastrophic impact you always assume it could have.

The feminine energy is powerful because it makes you feel powerful within yourself yet humbled in contrast to the power of the world. It gives you the courage to tap into what you want and know that whatever choice you make really only impacts the universe inside of you. Your decisions, your thoughts your emotions only impact you; they inhibit or empower you, no one else. And that is powerful.

Feminine energy is emotion, the ability to dream, the ability to feel in charge of your own universe, to understand yourself on a deeper level: your natural talents, the areas you need to work in, and the way you can create an environment customized to your needs so that you can succeed more effortlessly.

This energy is unleashed in the quiet time you make to THINK. Thinking time is priceless. It helps you tap into a world of clarity and really helps you solidify a relationship with yourself so that you can know on demand exactly what you need and desire and why.

Once you know what you need, you can later use your fiery energy to go out and achieve it. You will know exactly how to activate your drive and create a day that is purpose-driven and runs efficiently. But before you can effectively use your fire, you have to get in touch with that side of you that lies within your emotions.

For a long while, I underutilized this emotional energy because I thought it would make me seem weak or less than. I was too busy tapping into my masculine drive to accomplish and conquer that I lost sight of what was infinitely possible if I gave myself permission to think, feel and dream.

My mornings became filled with a little less physical exercise and a little more dream-conjuring. I streamlined my workouts to make extra space to write, journal, and read about how to tap into my emotions. These thirty to forty-five minutes a day became a superpower. It gave me the space to think, dream and expand my mind.

One room in my house had been empty for a while, and I decided to have a custom wall unit bookshelf built. It is filled with novels I've read because I enjoy reading fiction. But in 2022, I rearranged this room to be the room in which I manifest my dreams. I still call it my library, even though it's more of a reading and thinking room.

Every morning before sunrise, I sit at the window seat, staring out at the stars, and dream. I offer my gratitude for everything the universe has blessed me with, including the lessons I've learned. I journal about what I am working on, what I want to invite into my life, and how I am feeling about my evolution thus far.

My library is filled with empty journals. Whenever I see one with a cover that speaks to me, I buy it. And I fill them up just as fast as I buy them. I have one for gratitude, one for business-related ideas and goals, one for personal goals, and one for my daily random thoughts. I like to keep everything separated because that helps me go back to it more easily to reference when I'm in a particular mindset (though it's a pain in the butt when I'm traveling. I never know which to bring, so I usually just bring them all LOL).

Of course, crystals are also involved in my thinking ritual. I line my windowsill with crystals and affirmations that align with what I am working on at that moment. And I use all of my mental energy to envision the life I am trying to achieve while also showing immense gratitude for the life I've created thus far.

When you do these gratitude and visualization exercises, I recommend you get into as great of detail as you possibly can. I like physically putting pen to paper rather than using digital notes. First, it allows you to ignore technology during your visualization and thinking ritual. Second, there is no replacement for a physical connection between the ink and the journal. To me, it is more meaningful, more powerful energetically, and more impactful when you write something down with your hand. It is a connection between your more cerebral self in the mind and your more physical self in the body.

I bet you never thought that making time to think could be so powerful, huh?

This THINK TIME gave me the power to soar. It allowed me to gather all the thoughts, ideas, and creative energy inside of me and focus it all on building my dream life. It allowed me to reconnect to the power of hope.

Your vision for your life can only take flight if you create emotion and passion behind it. THINK TIME helps you to tap into those feelings so you can use them for greatness. It gets the mind flowing and the thoughts moving so that you can start to find that zest for life again.

Once you revive that passion inside of you, the world is yours to take over. And that takeover will require ACTION. Before we do a deep dive into action-taking, here are some quick tips on how to start getting that piece moving in the right direction.

I run two separate companies, speak on stage monthly, host events, write books, and publish articles monthly in Forbes and Entrepreneur, all while raising my two girls alone. I need to work with focus and efficiency in order to get it all done.

How? I create purpose-driven days and group my tasks by the energy I need to accomplish them. I was only able to do any of this because of the clarity I got during THINK TIME and gratitude-driven mornings.

Do not—I repeat, DO NOT—underestimate the impact and value that daily gratitude and visualization have on your actions.

Energy flows where your focus goes. Your mental focus will dictate your actions, even if you aren't actively aware of it. In the same way, if you buy a white car, suddenly you see them everywhere. Are there suddenly more on the road? No, of course not. But your mind is trained to see them now because purchasing your own white car is at the forefront of your mind.

When you start your day with gratitude and deep thought, your actions throughout the day will be more purposeful; they will have more intention behind them. You wake up every day and take care of business. You boss through the day.

But if you have the larger vision, purpose, and fulfillment at the forefront of your mind, imagine how much more impactful each action can be. Each thing you do throughout the day will push you ever so slightly toward the big dream you have in your life.

And instead of allowing every day to drag you in six directions as events unfold, you will be able to take control of the rhythm and make the most use of your 24 hours.

When I was thinking about what I needed and what I wanted, those elements of my life were at the forefront of my mind. So, as I went about my day, I was more aware of which parts of the day I was feeling more energized, focused, and efficient. I was also more aware of what tasks I was avoiding and which I was leaning into. I decided to take notes during the day of what lit me up the most, what I dragged my feet on the most, and what times of the day I was feeling the most empowered.

Some gurus call this a time study, but for me, it was really an energy study.

I found that I was the least productive when I kept switching gears. Now, that sounds so logical. You're probably like—duh, Jessica, we know multi-tasking isn't the answer.

But you guys are multi-tasking all day long. You make a laundry list of things to do, and then you bounce between them just to get stuff checked off. You're more concerned with paring down the list at all costs than effectively utilizing your brain power.

Grouping your tasks by energy will help you work through your day more effectively, with more enthusiasm, and in more alignment with your natural ebb and flow.

So how do you accomplish this? First, you observe. As I mentioned before (because I love Shakespeare), you must: Know Thy Self!

Let's get some logistics about your damn phone out of the way.

First things first, if you have any kind of audible sound coming from your phone—DISABLE that ISH immediately. And, take it a step further to put your phone on DND all the time. Do not take unscheduled calls. This was a game-changer for me. I also turned off all notifications from every app. I do app badge notifications only on certain apps related to my clients and staff; meaning, the app icon will show that I have an alert, but the alert won't pop up on my home screen and disrupt my flow).

Secondly, use a different app for your business than you do for personal. I have my barbershop staff on WhatsApp, my *Pivot & Slay* clients on Telegram, and my friends and family on text. That way, if I see a badge notification related to a working app, I will open it when I take a message-check break throughout the day. For friends and fam, I know that stuff can wait until I have the head-space to reply.

Ok, back to energy.

When I make my schedule for the week, I organize it by what type of energy I have to bring to the table. For example, every single Tuesday, I am in full-blown consulting mode. I start at 8:30 and do not end till five pm. I carve out thirty to sixty minutes for an eat-ing/thinking break, and other than that, I am in my mentor energy all day.

Why? Because if I am going to get into the mentoring mindset for one client, I might as well lean into that energy full throttle for the whole day. It takes less work for me to get into that mindset one time and maintain it throughout the day than to keep getting out and into it again throughout the week.

Same thing for writing, podcasting, or recording for YouTube/Reels/TikTok. If I get into one of those mindsets, I am staying there for the entire day.

Batching my energy helps me use my eight-hour days more ef-fectively. It helps me get more done in one day than most would get done in two days.

Another way I energy batch is to control my own calendar. As of right now, I will not send you a booking link. Instead, my team will book you on the calendar so that you butt up against another appointment. Nothing aggravates me more than inefficient use of time. If I have fifteen to thirty-minute intervals where I am on a "break," that isn't enough time for me to get anything productive done. Sending out booking links means the clients get to control what your hour blocks look like and how those blocks of time interact with one another. I'd rather ensure that my days are effective in a way that works best for me because that is how I can be my most impactful self for my staff, clients, and collaborators.

Protect your energy and make sure that you are running the show in a way that makes the most sense for you. Many of you panic, thinking a client should make the rules since they are paying you the big bucks. WRONG. Get selfish here, people. They are paying you great money because you're amazing at what you do. You are more amazing when you are working on your terms in a manner that is most meaningful and productive to you. So in order to give your clients their money's worth with the best version of you, make them schedule you on your terms, not theirs.

My last energy batch tip is to capitalize on the times of days when your brain power is most focused and alert. Some of us are spot on in the morning after our workouts, and some perform better in the evening. The time of day doesn't matter. Your awareness of it does matter. Take note of what tasks require the most energy from you, and then plan your day around doing those tasks at your peak brain power hour!

# Chapter 18

A vision is powerful, no doubt. We just devoted an entire chapter to learning how to dream and visualize all of the greatness you want to achieve.

But I don't want you stuck in the dreaming for too long. Dreaming is what unleashes the passion inside of you. It conjures up that excitable energy that gets you ready for Global Domination. But you cannot take over the world without ACTION.

Dreaming is a necessary step in the evolution of your life. Each time you are ready to evolve, you'll have to dream all over again. But a vision without action is meaningless.

Don't let my femininity fool you. Yes, I can harness all that "woo woo," hippie energy and write an entire chapter on how crystals and deep thinking under the moonlight have changed my life. But when the time comes to implement, my fiery sun side will emerge, ready to SLAY THE DAY®!

Emotion is what will get you to dream about the next level of life, but action is what you need to actually BUILD the next level of your dream life.

We each have both sides to us: the dreamer and the action taker. The feminine and the masculine. The Yin and the Yang. When I mentor others, I draw both out of you in rapid succession so that you aren't just stuck in the mesmerizing dream phase picturing your ideal life, but you're actually taking the steps necessary to achieve that life.

Dreaming creates space for you to get creative with your passion. Think of passion as the compass you need to find your direction in life. The compass just points to where you need to head. You still have to move your body in the direction the compass points. How do you move your body? You TAKE ACTION.

It took me a little while to get into a rhythm with my new routine. As I explained, I started small, slightly shifting my morning routine to not only include physical well-being but also steps in my spiritual and emotional evolution. Over the course of three or four months, I finally fell into a rhythm. The new way of thinking and feeding my soul became almost second nature, something I couldn't live without. And the benefits of this routine manifested themselves in small, minuscule ways. Tiny things eventually added up to a big shift in my life.

The dreaming and the visualization were taking root inside my soul, and it was seeping out here and there in the way that I spoke, acted, and started to align my life with the dream in the forefront of my mind.

In short, my constant focus on my larger vision shifted my actions without me even realizing it. I started to say NO more and more quickly to things and people that were not aligned with me. When I felt that pang of "this doesn't feel right," I just said no. I didn't overthink it or overanalyze why. I simply followed my gut.

**Free Resource Alert**: download a copy of my free ebook "Follow Your Instincts" at jessicadennehy.com.**

I did the same thing with decisions. Suddenly, I was saying yes to everything that felt aligned. If it felt right, I said yes. Sometimes without any further investigation. I was learning to trust myself, and this meant I would sometimes take massive action and make a commitment blindly. The funny part was it was all working out.

One glaring example I can think of was over the summer of 2022 when I got a random message from a Facebook follower I had never met. He said he was orchestrating an entrepreneur event in Brooklyn in a few weeks and wanted me to speak. I remember writing back—yes, I'd love to.

Days later, I realized I had just said yes to meeting a man I had never met in a loft in Brooklyn. Maybe not the best idea in theory, but it felt right. I took my brother to the event just to have another human with me, and we had the most amazing time. I got to speak not once but twice. We met a totally new group of people who ended up adding a lot of value to my life in various ways over the course of the next year. All because I said yes to something that felt right.

All of that morning, THINK TIME allowed me to get really clear on what I wanted my life to look like, who I wanted to be around, and what I wanted to accomplish. It gave me a greater connection to myself, so I could automatically act in a way that was most aligned with what I wanted. That was invaluable.

I started to take action in small ways that added up to massive change. The most notable way this became apparent was in my stage presence.

Remember, a few months prior I was struggling with infusing my energy into my speeches. I was up on stage with the strategies and the facts but without any emotion. That missing piece was the catalyst for me prioritizing myself and my THINK TIME. The more thinking I did, the more naturally my stage presence became more meaningful, emotional, and memorable.

It happened in phases. The first couple of times I spoke in 2022, I noticed moments during my fact-driven speech where I would let my emotion come out a little more. At that time, I was still scared to let anyone else see my passion, namely because I was not yet used to sharing it with the world. Like many people, I was afraid to say my message with emphasis and conviction because I was afraid of being judged. I was afraid that I would scare some people away by being too much or too passionate, or too direct.

In the time I spent connecting to myself, I slowly started to let go of the fear of being judged and realized it was only me judging myself. If I was happy with who I was and was able to live in my highest truth and good, then why should I care what anyone else said? This realization was an empowering shift in my perspective, and that power naturally started to shine through in my presence on stage.

It was subtle at first. I'd drip out some emotion during a piece of my presentation. I'd see the audience react positively to it, but I didn't quite know where to go from there. I just kept taking small action steps anyway. The next time I spoke, I would thread a little more emotion into parts of the tactical speech and see how the audience reacted to more emotion and a little less strategy.

Slowly over time, I began to really embrace my emotional side and squash my fears around sharing it. This made my stage presence more powerful, my speeches more impactful, and increased my influence over the audience. People in the crowd enjoyed my presentations more and started to recommend me to other people who were hosting events around the country. Suddenly, I was being asked to speak on stage more and more. It started with once a month and then increased to twice a month.

The more I stayed dedicated to my THINK TIME, the more effortlessly I was able to pop into action with both passion and energy. I started to say yes to any event that felt right just so I could get more practice. I also started prepping less before I got on stage. I left my notes behind and relied more on emotion to drive the direction and energy in the speech.

For a recovering control freak, this was a huge leap of faith. I was terrified that I would freeze or lose my train of thought or not be able to deliver to the audience with both an emotional connection to my story but also tangible strategies to implement.

Thus far, I have not failed. Relying on my passion is what has made me a more influential person and impactful speaker, and the proof of that is in the events I've been asked to present at.

It started with one women's event in particular. I'd say this event in Dallas was the very first time I was able to hop fully into my emotional self without editing, without worrying, and without any reservations.

I had never spoken to a room full of women before. My audiences were usually mixed but with a split that favored men by a large margin. That was because I was always living with my masculine energy. The doing, the achieving, the ego. I hadn't yet threaded in my emotional side.

This event in Dallas in April 2022 was the first time that I thought to myself: this is my chance to lean fully into my feminine energy and see what happens. It could have failed completely. I could have frozen up. It was something new and uncomfortable for me, but I intuitively knew this was my moment to take all that inner work I had been doing out for a test drive.

- Pause -

One surefire way to get me all emotional is to talk about my daughters. If you haven't figured it out yet, they are the two people I love most in this world, and not just because they are my kids.

The main reason I love them so much is because I genuinely connect with them and enjoy their company. I'm not just their mom. I'm their lifeline, the person they want to emulate, the person they come to when they're angry or mad or sad or happy. They are the people I've shared my lowest lows and highest highs with. And they are so damn intelligent, emotionally and otherwise. They remind me that I am human and doing the best I can every day and to love myself anyway.

We have a genuine connection that most people won't ever achieve with their kids. Maybe it's because it's just been the three of us for so long. Maybe it's because I create an environment of support, clarity, and awareness around them. Maybe it's because they are just naturally two amazing humans destined for greatness and born into this world with a purpose larger than life.

I don't know the answer. I don't understand it all, but I feel it all, and I lean into what I feel because now I'm cool like that and understand my emotional intuition.

- Unpause -

Ok, so now that we got that tangent out of the way, back to the story. I decided that to test drive this new emotional stage presence I'd bring my secret weapons: the girls. With them in the audience, I knew I would push myself harder to bring my A-ish game (just made that up, and I'm loving it). With them in the audience, I knew that telling my story would get even more emotional, and I would easily be able to lean into those feelings because my two biggest fans were watching me and cheering me on.

That speech changed my life and career forever. It was the culmination of all the hard work I had been doing on myself; of all the hustle I had put into the business thus far; and it was the moment in time that I will never forget when the direction of my business became ever so clear and for the first time in my entire life my mind, body, and soul were in complete alignment with the vision I had for my life, my business and my world.

I completely slayed it. And that isn't something I say often. I'm usually super critical of myself and take the smallest missteps and try to correct them for next time. But this particular speech was flawless. Not because it was actually flawless, but because it was the very first time I completely let my guard down on stage and just showed the audience every single ounce of who I was without any editing at all. I even teared up at the end when I looked at my daughters and said, "I told you I'd change our lives, didn't I?"

As vulnerable as I was up there, taking action based on only my emotion, I had never felt so powerful before. Being up in my feels didn't make me weak or open to criticism. It made me feel completely alive and in charge of my own destiny. It made me feel like I could do anything, and the look on my daughter's faces as they watched me close that speech said the same thing: we can take over this world, and dammit, we will!

Standing on that stage was a life-changing moment. I was completely in the zone telling the story of my second come up with so much emotion no one else in the room could change my energy. I created the energy in that room, and nothing else could shift it. When I finally made eye contact with someone, it brought my consciousness out of the zone and back to the room around me; I realized something. Everyone in that audience felt connected to me and my story. I did it. I invoked the passion, I made that human emotional connection to this group of 200 strangers, and I delivered a speech they would never forget that was also filled with valuable nuggets they could take away.

That moment is when I truly embraced my role in this world as a motivational speaker and made the commitment to myself to do more of this because it was the thing that lit me up the most. I never felt so fully ME, and to be accepted as my raw, authentic self by a room full of strangers just made me realize I had been hiding away for so long; it was time to unleash the goddess within me so that the world can see my light shine bright.

That was one of the best moments of my life. All because I got clear on me, got clear on what I wanted, and I used the energy of all my emotions to take action towards my dream life.

# Conclusion

That moment in Dallas was the first of many where I had an opportunity to impact large groups of people. It led me to who I am today and where I am today, both personally and in business. It started with THINK TIME. It soared with authenticity. And it solidified with intuitive action.

It all started a few months prior, with me getting selfishly devoted to my own happiness. With me creating the space in my life to connect with myself and find what lit me up the most. And with me staying dedicated to continuously leaning more and more into that connection with myself so I could continuously evolve and grow.

And with that small yet difficult step, I changed the course of my life forever.

Each area of my life started to get more expansive and gain more strength. Then, suddenly each of them started to thread together, unifying the complexity of who I am...all the roles, all the pieces of me becoming one dynamic human instead of a segregated compilation of tasks and functions.

The more complex and interesting I allowed my life to become, the more opportunity I received. No one wants a one-note boring person to speak on their stage or mentor them into success, or lead them as a CEO. People want to be around other people who can light them up and show them a happier and more dynamic way to live. People want to be around other people who inspire them to do bigger things.

Opportunities start to present themselves everywhere. Opportunity for me to be me, solidify all the relationships in my life and get more of what I was dreaming of.

I was asked to speak more frequently and at bigger events. Only two months after that Dallas appearance, I was offered a spot on the biggest stage of my career thus far. Nearly 3,000 people are in attendance at an arena when NHL teams take the ice. That moment would not have happened without the prior six months of hard inner work and selfish devotion to my happiness. I was also getting asked to speak on stage consistently twice a month all over the country, which gave me more opportunity to solidify my messaging and perfect my delivery (at least to the extent anything can really be perfect).

My relationship with myself continued to flourish as I got more clear on what lit me up and what I wanted to spend my time doing. By choosing to say yes to only things that felt aligned with who I am and what I wanted, I was able to dispel any feelings of guilt or stress over leaving the girls to travel, speak or work. Every time I said yes, I knew it was in furtherance of my highest truth, my highest good, and my highest purpose. And I knew that if I was in alignment with my highest purpose, my energy would be happy, enthusiastic, and bright, which would only make my family and home brighter.

I also showed up differently as a parent.

Because I was choosing the right opportunities that lit me up, I came home with enthusiasm and energy. I felt invigorated, and when I walked through the door, that energy was palatable. The girls lit up, even though they didn't quite understand why. I'd share with them the things I learned about myself while I was away doing my work things. I also shared with them the things I learned about myself during that introspective morning time I spent thinking.

I took them on the journey with me so that they would understand that every morning—I woke up before them at the crack of dawn instead of cuddling them a little extra because this ritual fortified our family. I took them on the journey with me so that they knew that every time I left the house for work or a work trip, it was because the experience I had there would somehow make our family life happier.

We hardly ever spoke about the financial aspect of it. They never asked if I was making more, if we had more, or if they could get more. The money wasn't the focus because the happiness was there. The larger purpose of strengthening our bond and of strengthening myself as a person was evident; they felt it in my presence. They saw it when I came home happier, when they came home from school to music blaring, me dancing in the kitchen while making pancakes for dinner. They felt that energy radiating from me, and they thrived off of it.

THAT happiness was the currency. THAT alignment was the money. THAT feeling of uninhibited freedom to be me was the value add that all my hard work was giving to the family because it helped the girls feel like they could go on in their daily lives living out their truth without apology.

The girls and I became closer than ever before. Our conversations were elevated to not only the run-of-the-mill daily tales of life but also to deeper meaningful, and emotional conversations. We spent time sitting on the counter eating dinner dreaming together about what fun stuff we could do, what adventures we could take, and how we could make more meaningful time for our family. And then, we actually changed those dreams into action.

The girls and I took several life-changing trips, including one to Iceland, where we got to explore a totally new country, culture, and sense of adventure we didn't know existed. We went snowboarding in the incredible mountains of Utah, swam under waterfalls in St. Lucia, and watched the Northern Lights dance across the sky in Iceland. We took a few trips to Disney, went horseback riding on lava fields, and submerged ourselves in natural mud baths. We started to live a life that lit us up together as a family. All because I redefined the word "selfish" and used it as a superpower.

By me getting clear on who I am and showcasing my true self to the world, I saw something change inside of the girls. They started dressing differently, for example. They started experimenting with style in a unique way, vastly different from their peers. Instead of worrying about what their classmates would say, they just go and be confident. The girls had this new energy about them where they were no longer afraid to speak their truth, not in an aggressive way, but in a way that let the world know what they would choose to tolerate and what they would not. I watched them navigate school and social situations with more grace and confidence, with more open communication, and with less regret. They started to trust themselves more and make decisions quickly without worrying about their mistakes.

That one speaking engagement in Dallas really gave me the fire inside to pursue public speaking as an avenue to grow *Pivot & Slay*. To give myself more opportunities to speak and connect, I created a FREE monthly entrepreneur event of my own each month in New York. This helped me not only perfect my craft on stage but also created a way for me to give back to the entrepreneurial community I loved so much.

This monthly event is a passion project for me. I wanted to create a space for entrepreneurs to receive high-level training from impactful industry leaders without a hefty price tag. The events are free, and I make zero dollars from them, but it brings me massive amounts of joy to help other business owners and create a community where they feel safe, heard, and supported.

It led me to meet my close friend and celebrity chef Eric Levine, who continuously motivates me to challenge myself and also generously donates his beautiful event space because he believes in my mission so deeply. The event also solidified some other business relationships with clients and other people in my circle who were looking for more opportunities to speak on stage. For those who didn't know where to start, I gave them an outlet to test a new skill set and speak in front of an audience for the first time as I mentored them through their first journey to the stage. These monthly events also give me an opportunity to inspire other entrepreneurs to grow their businesses and get devoted to themselves.

The *Pivot & Slay* Entrepreneur Meetup is all about giving because I believe that when you give the most, you also receive the most. Not only do the speakers pour into the community, but I've watched the attendees build deep connections with each other, which result in more business opportunities and collaborations. If you are ever in New York, be sure to attend one of these meetups by the Events tab at www.jessicadennehy.com. If you'd like to talk about setting up a meetup in your area, send me a follow and DM me on Instagram @thejessicadennehy.

Even though the *Pivot & Slay* Monthly Meetups were born out of a need for me to build a community and practice the art of public speaking, I found a way to make these events something that benefits everyone involved.

Learning to embrace selfish as a superpower may start with you, but remember: it is a lifestyle change that helps you fortify your relationship with yourself so that you can bring more energy and impact to the world!

Get devoted to what makes you happy so that you can radiate the light and positivity that will inspire others to take action that makes them happy. And that is the ripple effect of becoming selfishly devoted to your own happiness.

Turning inward and following my passions was a pivotal moment in my life that started to positively infiltrate every aspect of my life. I first saw the ripple effect come to life when my daughters started dreaming bigger as they saw me reaching for my big scary dreams.

This force was also evident as I watched the *Pivot & Slay* Entrepreneur Meetups, which not only created an opportunity for me to speak on stage but also for others to learn to build relationships and learn. Hosting the meetups every month as a labor of love also helped fortify my skill set as a business coach. Building a community of people that were truly united in helping each other lit me up and helped me bring back that passion and energy to my client base, which is all over the country. For those that couldn't come to the meetups in person, I took the knowledge from my speakers and attendees back to my consulting clients to help them in new ways. As I grew myself, my skill set matured and evolved into something more meaningful and valuable to everyone around me: my children, my clients, and even my staff.

Learning to embrace selfish as a superpower, rather than something negative, not only helped me build out my new business, but it also gave me an opportunity (and courage) to grow inside my first business—MadMen Barbershop. I was always afraid to be authentically me inside of that business since it was born from someone else's idea and not my own. As I entered the phase of my second come-up with *Pivot & Slay*, I was reluctant to share that with the barbershop staff. Even though I was no longer inside the daily grind at the shop, the staff knew MadMen was my singular focus. I thought they might feel slighted if they saw me traveling more and speaking more around the country. I thought they might feel less of a connection to me because my time was being filled-up with other things.

I couldn't be more wrong. I hit a point where I inevitably had to share my success with my social media audience, which meant some of my staff that followed me would see what I was up to. Their reaction was the exact opposite of what I had envisioned. They were not mad or upset with me. They didn't feel abandoned.

They felt inspired. They felt motivated. They felt encouraged. When I did go to the shop, I was more well-received than before.

They seemed to have gained a higher respect for me than they previously had because (I am guessing) I was sharing more of who I was with them rather than hiding it. I was speaking on Social Media and on stage about my expertise, which allowed them to see my value more clearly. Before, they weren't really sure what my role was in the company on a daily basis. They didn't automatically understand how I was contributing to the company because I never spoke to them about it. I would pop into the shops, ask about them, make sure things were running smoothly, and pop out.

Posting about my work at home, behind the scenes, and writing about the ways I helped build and fortify MadMen gave the staff a greater insight into my worth. The barbers also got a glimpse of who I am as a person because I was sharing that on social media, and it was also something I was not infusing into the shops when I was there. I would focus my energy and attention on them and not share with them anything about myself. The energy was flowing in only one direction, and while I had the best intention to be humble and not make the conversation about me, it was actually working against me because the staff couldn't connect with me on a human level.

Now that my life and my journey, and my thoughts were more publicized, they were able to feel that greater connection. They started to ask me questions about where I was traveling, what I enjoyed, what food I ate, how the girls were, etc. They were enjoying getting to know me, and I started to see them speak to me differently, share with me differently, and relate to me differently.

My connection to myself helped me connect more to the people I cared about, the businesses I cared about, my staff, my consulting clients, and my audiences both on stage and on social media.

My entire life changed.
My personal happiness.
My family dynamic.
My original business.
My new business.
My stage presence.
My daily routine.
My confidence.
My finances.
My inner peace.
My social media followings.
My soul purpose.
My relationship with self, family, kids, friends, clients, etc.

All because I chose me.

I chose to get to know myself and share that authentic side of me with the world.

All because I had the courage to embrace the fact that Selfish is a Superpower.

Photo Cred: Liz Degen Photography

# Ways to Work with Jessica

Visit www.jessicadennehy.com to:

- Book Jessica as a Keynote Speaker or TV Guest
- Book a Business Consultation with the *Pivot & Slay* Team
- Book Jessica as a Guest for Media Appearances or Podcasts
- Attend one of Jessica's Events
- Download Free Book Resources

Follow Jessica on all Social Media Platforms
@thejessicadennehy

# Acknowledgements

Emma & Quinn— You are the most amazing, magical people I know. Thank you for inspiring me to be the best version of myself, redefine the word selfish and write this book. You deserve the best mom and role model, and I will strive to be that each and every day. My hope is that through witnessing my journey first-hand, you will know that you can dream anything into existence if you want it bad enough and work hard enough. I have no doubt you will both take the world by storm in the best possible way, and I will be there to support you in the same enthusiastic, spirited way you support me. I love you both more than the whole world, and I am grateful every day the universe chose me as your mommy.

To my newest friend Michael Strahan, who taught me to say "when, not if." That surprise Zoom call with you changed the trajectory of my life forever. Thank you for encouraging me to believe in the impossible. No bee-sting cake could fully express my gratitude.

To Louis, I'm not sure how you came across my page or why you decided to share my message, but I am forever grateful. You are one of the funniest and most interesting people I've come across so far. I look forward to seeing your next book in print and cheering you on as the next chapters of your life unfold.

To the family and "family" who cheered me on through all the evolutions and iterations of me, even when they didn't quite understand what I was trying to accomplish. Even when I didn't call or text them back quickly enough or see them enough or remember the details of their life enough. Thank you for having patience with me and giving me the space and room to grow, and loving each version of me.

These people include my parents, John and Ann Marie. I love you more than I could ever express in words; my brother and sister-in-law Michael and Stephanie, who are the best aunt and uncle to my children and who I have the most fun with during our ultra-competitive sporting events, including Throw Throw Avocado (which is basically the Super Bowl of board games); my friend forever and ever since we were awkward 6th graders Kristen, who I couldn't live without. Thank you for loving me through all versions of me; my soul sister Stefanie who leaves me daily voice notes even when she knows I'm avoiding everyone because she wants me to know she's here for me and I appreciate that. We are meant for great things and I'm excited for all the adventures we are about to embark on; my friend Patty who understands all my nutty quirks as a mom and fully supports them. I am so grateful for our friendship; Amy, my work wifey, has become one of my closest friends. Your laughter is infectious and our adventures are endless. Our friendship is one of my favorites; Brian, thank you for encouraging me to take a chance on myself without guilt. Our stories are forever intertwined as an amazing time of growth, and Krista and Jen, who I am blessed to have on speed dial because your guidance is divine and full of amazing energy. Thank you for encouraging me to write this book!

To Amy and Ryan, who gave me that first opportunity to step on their stage in front of my girls and tell my story and who have given me many opportunities since. I am forever grateful!

And finally, my team....

Amber, thank you for all your hard work every day, especially through prepping the website for this book launch. I love working with you and my hope is that it never ends!

To Madi of 7 Seconds Media, who shot the amazing photo on the cover of this book and is responsible for almost all of my gorgeous branding pictures. You are magic!!! Your photos always showcase the best & brightest energy people have to offer.

BIG thank you to my publisher Tammy & publicist Suzi for taking a chance on crazy little me just because they saw my potential, the light in my eyes, and the passion in my voice. I appreciate your continuous effort on my behalf, your nudges in the right direction, and your sincere belief in the power inside of me. Thank you, thank you, thank you for helping me bring my dream to life.

# Author Bio

Jessica Dennehy is a best-selling author, dynamic speaker, and solo parent who is passionate about empowering others to push the boundaries of what's possible in their lives. From the moment she steps on stage, Jessica brings a level of excitement and enthusiasm that is truly infectious and leaves a lasting impact.

Jessica started her entrepreneurial journey over eleven years ago when she left her high-profile job as a Wall Street attorney to build a brand of luxury barbershops called MadMen. Unwilling to give up her ambitious career but also wanting to be the most present and involved parent she could be, Jessica carved out her path to having it all.

She learned to thrive and reconnect with her purpose and passions even through a painful divorce that left her as a solo parent, a major career change, and the stress of building multiple businesses.

With her diverse background, from business and entrepreneurship to personal development and self-improvement, Jessica is a powerhouse who knows how to captivate a crowd and inspire and energize audiences.

Jessica has been featured in Forbes, Entrepreneur Magazine, INC, Parade, Hello!, and more.

She lives in New York with her two beautiful daughters, and they love to travel and adventure worldwide. She believes a dynamic life should always include fun, family, and insatiable curiosity.

Photo Cred: **Liz Degen Photography**